PROJECTS AND PRESENTATIONS

THE
WORLD
BOOK

Volume
6
PROJECTS
AND
PRESENTATIONS

Published by
World Book, Inc.
a Scott Fetzer company
Chicago

Staff

Publisher
William H. Nault

Editorial

Editor in Chief
Robert O. Zeleny

Executive Editor
Dominic J. Miccolis

Associate Editor
Maureen M. Mostyn

Senior Editor
Michael K. Urban

Writer
Kathleen L. Florio

Production Editor
Elizabeth Ireland

Index Editor
Joyce Goldenstern

Permissions Editor
Janet T. Peterson

Editorial Assistant
Elizabeth Lepkowski

Art

Executive Art Director
William Hammond

Designers
Tessing Design, Inc.

Photography Director
John S. Marshall

Photographers
Don Sala
Jim Ballard

Product Production

Executive Director
Peter Mollman

Manufacturing
Joseph C. La Count, director

Research and Development
Henry Koval, manager

Pre-Press Services
Jerry Stack, director
Randi Park
Sandra Van den Broucke

Proofreaders
Marguerite Hoye, head
Ann Dillon
Esther Johns
Daniel Marotta

Copyright © 1986 by
World Book, Inc.
Merchandise Mart Plaza
Chicago, Illinois 60654

Printed in the United States of America

ISBN 0-7166-3190-3 (Volume 6)
ISBN 0-7166-3184-9 (set)
Library of Congress Catalog No. 86-50558
c/hg

Contents

Introduction 7

Section I
Presenting Your Project—
and Yourself 8

Section II
Developing Your Project 14

Section III
Rehearsing Your Presentation 48

Section IV
Making Your Presentation 78

Section V
Ideas for School Projects 90

Section VI
Attention Getters 112

Index 124

Acknowledgments

The anecdote on Inca ruins that appears on pages 116–117 was adapted from *Secrets of the Past* by Gene S. Stuart, copyright © 1979, National Geographic Society.

The quotation from Carl Sagan that appears on pages 121–122 is from *Cosmos* by Carl Sagan, copyright © 1980 by Carl Sagan Productions, Inc. Reprinted by permission of the author and the author's agents, Scott Meredith Literary Agency, Inc., 845 Third Avenue, New York, New York 10022 and Random House, Inc.

Introduction

From time to time in school you are called upon to create a special project or to deliver an oral presentation as part of your classwork. Such a situation provides you with an opportunity to be creative and to share what you learn with your fellow classmates. *Projects and Presentations* tells you how to put together projects and present them effectively to your audience.

The first section of this volume explains why projects and presentations are an important part of your schoolwork. It also describes the types of skills that you develop by performing such assignments. The second section gives helpful information on developing your project, from analyzing your audience to making props and using audio-visual aids.

Section III helps you rehearse your presentation. It offers various delivery techniques and gives a step-by-step approach to your rehearsals. Section IV tells you what to do on the day of your presentation. Helpful hints explain how to handle stage fright, audience reaction, and unexpected problems.

The fifth section of *Projects and Presentations* contains more than 100 ideas that you can use for school projects. There are suggestions for each major area of study: social studies, science, language arts, and math. The final section of this volume explains how to get your audience's attention and hold it by using helpful speaking devices such as anecdotes, quotations, questions, and startling facts.

Before you begin your next class project or presentation, consult this volume. You will get the extra help you need in order to make your assignment a success that benefits both you and your schoolmates.

This section explains the purpose of creating projects and presentations and the skills you will need to develop in order to carry out these assignments.

The Purpose of Your Project   10

The Long-Term Benefits   13

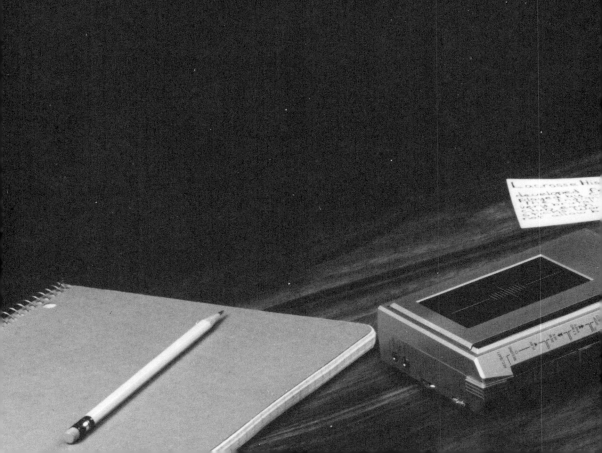

Presenting Your Project—and Yourself

A s a student, your day-to-day school learning experience is shaped in many ways. You spend time reading textbooks, listening to teacher lectures, participating in class discussions, doing homework, and taking part in all sorts of other learning activities. Some of the most challenging of these learning activities involve projects and presentations.

Doing a project means creating something—an object or an event. For example, you might make a model or a diorama, sculpt a figure, demonstrate a folk dance, or dramatize a scene from a story. Presentations are the means by which you share your project with your classmates or some other audience. In most cases, you simply stand in front of the class to present your project. At other times, you present your project to a group outside your classroom—other students or parents, for example. Sometimes, as in dramatic reading, the presentation and the project are the same thing.

Projects and presentations fit into the school routine in a variety of ways. They may be assigned to everyone in the class as part of the regular curriculum. Your social studies teacher, for example, may ask you and your classmates to do projects as you study a unit on Latin America. Sometimes you do a project—either assigned or voluntary—for a special school activity, such as a science fair. You may do a project for extra credit to help save a grade from tumbling. On certain occasions, your class may work together on a project that will be presented as a program for parents or the entire school.

The Purpose of Your Project

Doing a project and preparing a presentation can take a considerable amount of time. It is time well spent, however, because in the process you are gaining knowledge, tapping your creativity, and developing skills that will come in handy both in and out of school.

Helping You Learn

Even the best teachers cannot give you all the information they would like to about certain topics. There just is not enough time. Projects give you and your classmates a chance to learn more than what can be taught in the limited amount of time your teacher spends with you each day. Learning does not stop when you step out of the classroom, and doing a project is a form of independent study—learning on your own. When it is your turn to present your project, you are giving your classmates information they may not have known before. As you listen to your classmates present their projects, you are learning from their experience and effort. In this way, each of you contributes to the overall learning process.

Projects can be particularly effective learning tools, because they make you, the student, an active participant in the learning process. In many cases, projects involve a hands-on approach to learning. For example, instead of just reading in your science textbook about the properties of air, you can set up a demonstration showing that air weighs something or that hot air rises. By doing, instead of just reading or listening, you are more likely to remember what you have learned.

Tapping Your Interests and Creativity

For many students, projects are a lot of fun to do. They give you a chance to pursue a special interest or satisfy a curiosity. Perhaps you are interested in drama, and you would like to find out what theaters looked like in Shakespeare's time. Building a model of the Globe Theatre might be an acceptable project for your English class and an enjoyable experience at the same time.

Because many projects involve a creative process, they frequently give you a chance to put special talents or hobby skills to good use. If you love to work with clay, for example, and you are studying American Indians in your social studies class, a project assignment might mean a chance to create a bowl or a pitcher in the style of the Zuni Indians.

Skills You Will Develop

In addition to the learning and the fun involved in doing projects and presentations, you will develop a number of important skills in the process. These include the skills necessary to do research, to organize information, to speak before a group, and to work cooperatively with others.

Research Skills

As you plan and create a project, you will develop research skills. You cannot build a model of the Globe Theatre or create a Zuni bowl without first finding out what those things look like. Your project may lead you to the library to find information or to other sources that can provide you with the facts you need.

Organizing Skills

As you prepare for the presentation of your project, you need to organize the facts at hand so that you can present them in a way that makes sense and that your classmates can follow easily. These organizing skills are an important part of a successful presentation.

Speaking Skills

When you present your project, one of your main purposes is to share what you have learned with your audience.

Making a presentation involves another set of skills—speaking skills. When you present your project, one of your main purposes is to share what you have learned with your audience. You need to convey your message clearly and keep the audience's attention from start to finish. To do that, you must employ the techniques of effective public speaking. Learning how to speak in front of a group involves more than just saying words, however. It also means having poise and self-confidence. In that sense, you are presenting yourself, as well as your project, when you stand up to make your presentation.

Socialization Skills

If you are doing a group project, you have an opportunity to develop the socialization skills needed for successful co-operation. Working as part of a group is different from preparing a project and presentation on your own. It calls for sharing ideas, dividing responsibilities, and doing your part to assure that the final effort succeeds.

The Long-Term Benefits

When your school years are behind you, you may not remember every project and presentation you made as a student. But the skills you developed can continue to serve you in various ways.

The student who was able to think of a good project idea, gathered and organized the necessary information, and then presented it effectively may grow up to be the adult who is asked to take on additional job responsibilities and leadership roles. In many career areas, success depends on creative thinking, diligent research, and self-confident presentations.

These same skills can help you become an active, involved member of a civic organization or a community group. Knowing how to carry through a project from start to finish is an asset whether you are planning a PTA fundraiser, organizing a neighborhood movement for improved community services, or working to elect a political candidate. Communicating with poise and confidence enhances your involvement even further.

Projects and presentations add a special dimension to your school life by allowing you to express yourself in a variety of ways. They allow you to be creative and resourceful and to interact with others. Take advantage of the opportunities they present. Learn from them, enjoy doing them, and remember that the skills they help you develop can provide lifelong benefits.

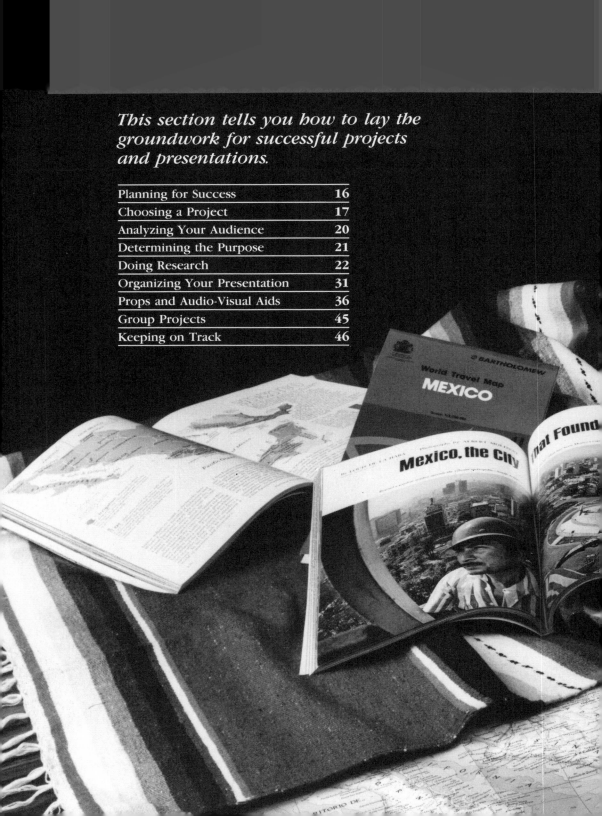

This section tells you how to lay the groundwork for successful projects and presentations.

Planning for Success	**16**
Choosing a Project	**17**
Analyzing Your Audience	**20**
Determining the Purpose	**21**
Doing Research	**22**
Organizing Your Presentation	**31**
Props and Audio-Visual Aids	**36**
Group Projects	**45**
Keeping on Track	**46**

Developing Your Project

*P*art of the appeal of projects is their variety. A
social studies class of thirty students may come
up with thirty different ideas for a project on
*Japan. Each can be successful in its own way, provided
the creator puts·in the necessary time for planning and
development. Good projects come in different shapes
and sizes, but they all reflect a certain amount of hard
work.*

Planning for Success

Some projects are more complicated than others and involve more time and effort. Some require extensive research, while others rely largely on information you already have at hand. Some involve making a model that
takes several days or even weeks of careful craftsmanship;
others consist of things that can be easily assembled from
ready-made materials. Some projects call for lengthy rehearsals of the presentation; others may call for you to
think on your feet and make up your presentation as you
go along.

When you get an assignment to do a project, resist
the temptation to put off doing anything about it. It is all
too easy to become lax about getting started, especially if
you have several weeks to complete the assignment. You
may say, "But I've got four weeks to come up with something. Why should I worry about it right away?" Stop and
think. Chances are, if your teacher has given you four or
five weeks in which to complete a project, he or she probably will expect something that reflects an effort made over
that amount of time.

Instead of burying the assignment somewhere in
your notebook or backpack and forgetting about it, make
an effort on the very first day to get yourself organized.
Think carefully about all the steps that will be involved
from start to finish. Plan your time carefully to assure suc-

cess. It may take a while just to decide what kind of project you want to do. You need to think about the audience you will be presenting your project to, and you must determine just what you want to accomplish with your project. You probably need to do research of some sort and then organize the information you find for your presentation. Perhaps you need to make some visual aids or props for the presentation. And, of course, you need to practice the presentation so it goes smoothly.

You may find it helpful to make a day-by-day schedule to guide your work. Be realistic in figuring how much time you need for each step. Allow for some leeway in case unexpected problems occur, and don't forget to consider assignments you have in other classes. Because of homework and other commitments, you may not be able to spend more than an hour or two a day working on your project and presentation.

Once you have made a satisfactory schedule, do your best to stick to it. Check off your progress as you move from one step to the next. If you are diligent about meeting your preliminary deadlines, you will save yourself a lot of agony the night before the project is due.

Choosing a Project

Unless your teacher tells you specifically what to do, choosing a project can be difficult. The possibilities are practically endless. You need to consider various factors as you narrow the possibilities and make your decision. Some of the things you should think about as you make your choice include your own personal interests and background knowledge, your particular talents and abilities, the availability of project materials, how much time you have to work on the project, and possible time limits on the presentation.

Personal Interests and Background Knowledge

What do you like to do? What are you really interested in? Is there something you already know a little bit about that you would like to explore further? Ask yourself these questions as you begin to think about your project, and then choose a project that fits. You may be spending several weeks working on your project, so you should try to make it as enjoyable as you can. Besides, you will probably do a much better job working on something that really interests you. When it comes time to give your presentation, your enthusiasm for the topic can make a real difference in the effectiveness of your delivery. Your audience is likely to be much more interested in what you have to present if you appear excited about it.

You will probably do a much better job working on something that really interests you.

Sometimes it takes a while to figure out how to make a project fit your interests. Let's say that you are assigned to do a project in chemistry, which is not your favorite subject. Maybe you enjoy taking pictures, though, and you have some darkroom experience. Why not consider a project on darkroom chemistry? You might be able to do a display or a demonstration showing the role chemistry plays in the developing and printing of film.

This example also shows how you can take advantage of background knowledge—things you already have some familiarity with, either through hobbies, extracurricular activities, or other experiences. It may not always be possible to put your background knowledge to work on a project, but it is a factor you should definitely consider.

Putting Your Talents to Good Use

As you consider various project possibilities, think objectively about your talents. What are you really good at doing? Perhaps you are all thumbs when it comes to arts and crafts, but you have an excellent speaking voice. If you have to do a project on mythology for your English class, you might decide to select one or more myths and tell them aloud. Your classmate who has a knack for working with clay, on the other hand, might choose to sculpt a mythological figure.

Even the same project can be handled in various ways, depending on your individual abilities. Suppose that you and two of your classmates each decide to build models of a medieval castle. Perhaps you build the structure out of wood and cover it with paint mixed with sand to resemble the rough surface of a stone castle. One of your classmates might use clay to shape walls, towers, and turrets. The other classmate might build a castle out of cardboard cartons, oatmeal boxes, and paper cones. All three projects can be successful, but they use very different materials, depending on the abilities of the student creators.

Be sure to analyze your strong points and take advantage of them when you choose a project. Don't plunge into something that will be difficult for you to complete successfully.

On the other hand, don't underestimate your abilities. Don't eliminate a tempting project idea until you are sure there is no way you can handle it. If you have difficulty drawing, you might still be able to create an attractive poster or illustration by making a collage with pictures cut from magazines and lettering done with stencils or stickers.

Availability of Materials

Your project will not get off the ground if you cannot find the materials you need to do it. Before you settle on a topic choice, check to make sure that all the things you need are readily available. Don't, for example, decide to prepare an authentic Peruvian dessert if your community doesn't have a grocery store that stocks all the necessary ingredients.

Time Allotted

Consider how much time you have to do your project, and then choose a project you can realistically accomplish in that time. If you are thinking about doing a model for a history project on ancient Greece, do you really have time to construct a model of the entire Acropolis, or should you consider building a miniature temple instead? Try to limit your plans to something you can do really well, rather than tackling a large-scale project that ends up looking sloppy because you had to rush to finish it all.

Presentation Time Limits

If your teacher has placed a time limit on how long your presentation can be, take that into consideration as you choose a project. If you have ten minutes for your presentation, and you want to do a dramatization from *Huckleberry Finn,* choose a single scene rather than trying to condense the entire story.

Analyzing Your Audience

A good speechwriter knows that it is important to analyze the intended audience before preparing a speech. When you are planning a project and presentation, you should go through a similar process. Think about who is going to view your project and watch your presentation, and tailor it to fit your audience. You need to consider such factors as age, education level, the audience's familiarity with the topic, and the size of the audience.

Think about who is going to view your project and watch your presentation, and tailor it to fit your audience.

Age and Education Level

You want to make sure that your audience understands what your project is about and that you can hold their interest during your presentation. People of different ages and education levels differ in their ability to understand ideas. If you are going to present your project to a class of seventh graders, your approach would be different than if you were going to present it to a group of first graders. You may need to adjust your vocabulary and otherwise simplify your presentation for the first-grade group. If you are presenting your project to a group of parents, on the other hand, you can probably use more technical language.

Similarly, a young audience will have a shorter attention span than an older audience. Keep your presentation brief for a young audience.

Familiarity with the Topic

Take into consideration how much your audience already knows about the topic when you make your presentation. Suppose that your class has been studying West Africa, and you are presenting a project on different kinds of housing in that region. Most likely, you would not have to include as much explanatory background information in a presentation to your classmates as you would if you were presenting your project to a group of parents who are probably not very familiar with life in West Africa.

Size

The size of your audience can sometimes affect the kind of project you do. If your audience is small, your project can also be small-scale. If you are going to construct a model of the human heart and show it to your biology class as part of a presentation on how the circulatory system functions, you could make a small model that sits on a desk or table top. But if you are going to make your presentation on stage in the school auditorium, you might decide to do a series of large diagrams of the heart, instead.

Audience size can also affect the tone and structure of your presentation. In general, a large audience requires a more formal, carefully structured presentation than a small audience.

Determining the Purpose

Most projects and presentations provide people with information. Their purpose is to inform the audience. A model of the solar system, for example, may provide information about the relative sizes of the planets and their locations in relation to the sun.

Projects may have two other purposes. They may entertain the audience, or they may persuade the audience to do something or accept an idea. A class program that demonstrates European folk dances is an example of a project intended to entertain the audience. If you prepare a science project that consists of a series of posters to discourage teen-agers from smoking, the purpose of your project is persuasion.

A project often serves more than one purpose. The class presentation of European folk dances may not only entertain, but it may provide the audience with information about the origins of the dances or some other aspect of the topic.

Doing Research

The information you convey in your project and presentation must be accurate, and that generally means doing some research. Even if you think you already know a lot about your topic, research may turn up new information or give you ideas for a different approach to your project. Thorough research will also give you the self-confidence you need for a smooth presentation.

There are a number of different ways to go about doing research. The library may be the first place that comes to mind. It can provide all the information you need for many projects. If you are having a hard time even thinking of a project to do, browsing through books in the library can help trigger ideas. Other ways to do research include firsthand observation, conducting an interview, or writing to government agencies, professional associations, or other groups.

Thorough research will give you the self-confidence you need for a smooth presentation.

Using the Library

Getting to know the library—and the librarians—makes research assignments much easier. If you are not already familiar with the various sections of your school and public libraries, take the time to get acquainted. Learn where nonfiction books are kept, including reference works, such as encyclopedias and atlases. Familiarize yourself with the procedures for getting magazines and newspapers. Discover what other sorts of materials are available to library users. Many library collections include art prints, maps, records, audiotapes and videotapes, filmstrips, slides, and movies. In addition, your library may have equipment that you can borrow for your presentation, such as movie and slide projectors or video and tape recorders.

The Library Catalog

In most cases, you should begin your library research by checking the library catalog. The catalog lists every book the library contains and gives the call numbers that help you locate the books on the shelves. Library catalogs come in various forms. Traditional card catalogs consist of file cabinets filled with cards filed in alphabetical order according to book titles, authors, and subjects. Other catalogs are in book form or on microfilm. Some libraries have computerized catalogs.

You may be thinking, "Why bother to look in the catalog? Isn't it easier to just go to the shelves?" It may be easier, but it is definitely not the smartest approach to take. If you skip the catalog and just head for the shelves, you are going to get an incomplete picture of the library's collection, and you may miss out on a book that would be a terrific source for your project.

Keep in mind that there are many books that the library owns that are not on the shelves because someone has checked them out or because they need to be reshelved. By checking in the catalog first, you know exactly what the library has to offer. If you don't find the book you want on the shelf, ask the librarian to find out if it has been checked out. If it has, you can ask the library to put the book on reserve for you. Then, you will be notified when the book is returned, and you can check it out. If the book is simply on a cart waiting to be reshelved, you can usually check it out immediately.

Unless you have a specific book title or author in mind when you begin to look through the library catalog,

Try to look at your topic from various perspectives so that you don't accidentally miss a good source.

it is best to start by looking up the subject you are interested in. Try to look at your topic from various perspectives so that you don't accidentally miss a good source. For example, if you are thinking about making a traditional Nigerian mask, you might begin your research by looking under the subject heading *Nigeria*. But there may be other helpful books listed under such headings as *Masks, Costumes, Crafts, Sculpture,* or *Papier-Mâché*.

When you find a book title that looks promising, copy down the call number that appears in the catalog entry. Call numbers are assigned to every nonfiction book and are used to organize the books into subject categories.

Most libraries use the Dewey Decimal Classification System to classify nonfiction books. In this system, books are numbered according to these ten main classes or subject areas:

000–099 General works (encyclopedias, bibliographies, and periodicals)
100–199 Philosophy and related disciplines (psychology, logic, and ethics)
200–299 Religion
300–399 Social sciences (political science, economics, law, and education)
400–499 Language (dictionaries, grammar, and linguistics)
500–599 Pure sciences (mathematics, astronomy, physics, chemistry, biology, and botany)
600–699 Technology (medicine, engineering, agriculture, business, radio, and television)
700–799 The arts (architecture, sculpture, painting, and music)
800–899 Literature (novels, poetry, and plays)
900–999 History and geography

If you come across a call number with the letters R or REF in front of it, it means that the book is located in the reference section of the library. Books in the reference section may not be checked out; they must be used within the library.

The Vertical File

Libraries keep brochures, pamphlets, newspaper and magazine clippings, pictures, and similar items in a vertical file. The file generally consists of file cabinets with folders arranged in alphabetical order according to subject. It may be worth checking the vertical file to see if your subject has a folder.

Periodical and Newspaper Indexes

If you are looking for up-to-date information, newspapers and magazines may be the best sources available. Check *The Readers' Guide to Periodical Literature* to find out if there are magazine articles about your topic. The *Readers' Guide* indexes articles from more than 100 major non-technical magazines. Entries are listed in alphabetical order according to subject and author and are sometimes also listed by title. Other periodical indexes, such as the *Art Index,* cover special-interest magazines not included in the *Readers' Guide.*

The *New York Times Index* provides a complete index to articles that appear in the *New York Times* newspaper. Libraries throughout the country subscribe to the *New York Times* because of its extensive coverage of national and international news and its feature articles on science, health, the arts, and many other topics. If your library has the *New York Times* available, a check through the index may turn up useful information.

Be sure to ask the librarians for help if you are having a hard time finding information of any sort. They often can turn up sources you haven't thought of looking for.

Library Services

In addition to materials, find out what sorts of special services your library offers. Many libraries offer a telephone information, or reference, service that provides quick answers to research questions. You simply call the library with your question, and a reference librarian looks up the answer for you. You should not abuse this service by relying on it to take the place of your own research. But it can come in handy if you need a quick fact and cannot get to the library yourself.

Some libraries provide computer-assisted research through the use of information services, which are also called online database systems. Information services consist of a huge database—a collection of information—stored in a central computer and a transmittal system that allows outside users to tap the database via telephone hookups with their own computers. If your library subscribes to an information service, the librarian can use the library's computer to retrieve research information for you from the central database. The research information may consist of a bibliography that lists various sources dealing with a particular topic, or it may consist of actual summaries or reprints of articles.

Firsthand Observation

Sometimes the best way to do research is through firsthand observation of a process, an event, or an object. For example, you might visit a museum to look at an exhibit of American Indian craft items before you attempt to make a feathered headdress of your own. If your project consists of a demonstration of how water in your community is purified, visit the local filtration plant and observe the process in person.

In many cases, it is wise to call first to make arrangements for your visit. You might be able to have a guide accompany you on your tour through the museum exhibit and answer any questions you may have. Places like the water filtration plant may require that arrangements be made in advance. A quick phone call can save you the frustration of arriving only to find out that the facility is not open to the public.

It is a good idea to jot down notes or make drawings as you do your observation. Don't rely on your memory alone for all the details. Find out if there are any pamphlets or other printed material available that you can take with you when you leave.

Interviews

Interviews can provide you with expert opinions, personal viewpoints, or facts that might be hard to track down elsewhere. For example, if you were preparing an original drama tracing the history of your community, you might want to interview elderly people who have lived in the area for many years.

The person you interview should have firsthand knowledge of the topic or be otherwise qualified. To conduct a successful interview, you should also follow these guidelines:

The person you interview should have firsthand knowledge of the topic or be otherwise qualified.

1. Request an interview by calling the person or writing a letter and following up with a phone call. During your phone call or in your letter, identify yourself, describe your project, and tell the person exactly what sort of information you are looking for. Agree to meet at a time convenient to the person you are interviewing.

2. Do some background reading so that you can ask intelligent questions, and prepare a list of questions beforehand.

3. Arrive for the interview promptly.

4. Take notes, or if the person agrees, use a tape recorder. Be sure to ask for the spelling of unfamiliar words or names.

5. At the end of the interview, review any areas you are unsure of to avoid errors and misunderstandings.

6. Thank the person, and follow up with a written thank-you note.

Questions for Interview

1. When did you first become involved in politics?

2. How does the job of town commissioner affect your personal and professional life?

3. What do you feel your major accomplishments have been since taking office?

4. What stand do you take on the proposed sub-development to be built next to the railyards? Why?

5. What plans do you have for attracting industry to this area?

Writing for Information

Many projects can benefit from information provided by government agencies, business organizations, or professional associations. These groups publish a tremendous variety of pamphlets, information bulletins, newsletters, and other materials that are available to the public—often free of charge.

Avoid Disappointment

Make your written requests for information as soon as possible after receiving your project assignment.

Keep in mind that it may take several weeks to get a reply when you write for information. You should not rely on a distant source if you only have a short time to complete your project. Make your written requests for information as soon as possible after receiving your project assignment. Tell the recipient what your project is about and exactly what kind of information you need. Include a large self-addressed, stamped envelope with your request to make it easy for the recipient to reply promptly.

Sometimes the information you receive is not exactly what you expected. That is why it is always best to have other sources of information at hand to fill in the gaps if necessary. You can also avoid disappointment by calling first to find out if the information you need is available and if the source you are planning to contact is, in fact, the right one. You don't want to waste valuable time as your request is passed from one department to another.

Writing to U.S. Government Agencies

The federal government publishes information on everything from solar energy to gold mining. You can find the addresses of U.S. government agencies by looking in *The United States Government Manual,* a book that is available in most libraries. Direct your request to the public affairs office or the public information office of the agency you are writing to. A librarian can probably help you decide which agency would be an appropriate source for the information you are seeking.

Most libraries also have lists of government publications that are available to the public. The most helpful lists are the *Monthly Catalog of United States Government Publications* and *Selected United States Government Publications*. Browse through these lists in search of specific titles that pertain to your topic.

State and Local Agencies

State and local government agencies can provide information about population statistics, economic resources, tourist attractions, and many other topics. Look in your telephone directory for the addresses and phone numbers of these agencies. If state agencies are not listed in your local telephone directory, check the library for your state capital's telephone directory.

Local chambers of commerce, tourist information centers, and visitor centers can also provide certain kinds of information. Travel guides often include the addresses and phone numbers of these organizations. Many other agencies, such as public utilities, publish booklets, pamphlets, and other informative items as a public service. A simple phone call to the public relations department or customer service department may turn up all the information you need. Again, check your local telephone directory to find the names, addresses, and phone numbers.

Business and Professional Associations

Business and professional associations are additional sources you can write to for information. There are thousands of such organizations, and you may find one that can provide valuable information on your topic. Check to see if your library has a copy of the *Encyclopedia of Associations,* which lists the addresses and phone numbers of thousands of associations. Your librarian may be able to point out other helpful directories.

Organizing Your Presentation

Projects and presentations go hand in hand. When you do a project, you are usually expected to share it with your classmates or some other audience. If you have spent a lot of time creating a successful project, you should take pride in presenting it effectively.

Your Goals

When you make a presentation, you should have two goals in mind:

1. Convey information clearly.

2. Hold the interest of your audience from start to finish.

The first goal should be an obvious one. Your presentation will not succeed if the audience cannot understand what you are talking about. But even a presentation that is easily understood will fall short if the audience is bored. You need to work on achieving both goals in order to have a successful presentation.

Kinds of Presentations

If you have spent a lot of time creating a successful project, you should take pride in presenting it effectively.

Project presentations can take various forms. Some are very informal and spontaneous. At a science fair, for example, you may simply be standing next to your project, and when an interested observer stops to look at it, you explain what it is, how it works, and what you found out.

There are also situations in which the presentation and the project are one and the same. An example would be a dramatic reenactment of a historical event. In this case, your project involves doing research and creating a script, but the presentation is the main focus of the project.

Most presentations fall somewhere in between. For example, you make a model of a Civil War battlefield and then discuss it in front of your class. This kind of presentation is really an oral report, and it should follow a well-organized format similar to that for a written report. The rest of this section tells how to go about organizing this kind of presentation.

Pinpointing Your Purpose

Begin planning your presentation by pinpointing your purpose. Decide exactly what you will try to achieve when you make your presentation. As you focus on your purpose, keep two things in mind:

1. Be specific.

2. Keep your purpose within an attainable range.

Here are examples of statements of purpose that violate both of these guidelines:

1. I will tell my audience about the Revolutionary War.

2. I will tell my audience about minerals.

3. I will tell my audience about Hopi Indian crafts.

All of these statements are far too general, and they represent impossible tasks for a project presentation. A person could talk for days about the Revolutionary War, minerals, or Hopi Indian crafts and not cover all aspects of the topic.

Here are rewritten versions of the statements that do a better job of specifying an attainable purpose:

1. I will tell my audience about the kinds of weapons used by the American colonists during the Revolutionary War.

2. I will show my audience how to cut and polish four different kinds of common minerals.

3. I will tell my audience about the significance of Hopi Indian kachina dolls and show how they are made.

Each of the revised statements is specific. You know exactly what to expect in the presentation. And the goals are attainable. The presenter should be able to cover the specified topic within a reasonable amount of time.

The Three-Part Structure

Once you have pinpointed your purpose, you are ready to organize the structure of your presentation. A well-organized presentation should have three parts: an introduction, a body, and a conclusion. Each part has a particular role to play, but they all work together to create a successful presentation. In addition, they all must relate to the purpose of your presentation.

A well-organized presentation should have three parts: an introduction, a body, and a conclusion.

The introduction to your presentation establishes your purpose. It lets the audience know what you are going to talk about, and it also should immediately arouse their interest. Don't begin a presentation by saying, "Now I will tell you about . . ." or, "My project was to . . . ." Try instead to think of a way to make your audience sit up and pay attention to what you are about to say. Maybe a startling statistic or a question posed to the audience will do the trick.

The body of your presentation is the longest part. In it, you share the information you gathered while you worked on your project. In most cases, the body consists of one or more main points along with a number of supporting details.

You can choose various ways to present the main points of your presentation. You can arrange them in order of importance, going from most important to least important. Some presentations use a chronological approach in which you describe events in the order in which they occurred. Certain kinds of presentations, such as demonstrations, can use a step-by-step approach. If you are explaining something that is complicated or difficult to understand, begin with the simplest points and work up to the more complex ones.

Be careful not to let yourself wander as you develop the body of your presentation. All of the information you present should relate to the purpose you have stated in the introduction.

The conclusion should summarize what you have said before. But it is also your last chance to impress the audience. Try to leave them with something they will remember in a positive way.

There is an easy way to remember the three-part structure of a presentation. Just think of it like this:

1. Tell them what you're going to tell them.
2. Tell them.
3. Tell them what you told them.

Attention Getters

Even a well-organized presentation can fall flat if it fails to hold the audience's attention. There are various devices you can use to keep the audience alert and interested. These include anecdotes, quotations, startling statistics, and audience participation. These attention getters can be worked into any part of your presentation—introduction, body, or conclusion. Section VI presents examples of various attention getters and tells how to use them effectively in a presentation.

Even a well-organized presentation can fall flat if it fails to hold the audience's attention.

Preparing an Outline

If your presentation includes a lot of information, one of the best ways to organize it beforehand is to prepare an outline that lists the main points you plan to cover. The outline can consist of a simple list, or it can follow the format you would use in preparing a formal outline for a written report or term paper. In either case, the major points should be listed in the order in which you intend to present them. Here is an example of an outline for a presentation on Hopi Indian kachina dolls:

I. Religious significance
   A. Associated with male kachina ceremonial dancers
   B. Represent supernatural beings—messengers to the gods
      1. More than 200 different kinds
      2. Identified by symbols, colors, shapes of body parts, and other markings
II. Function—to teach children as part of their religious training

III. How kachina dolls are made and decorated
    A. Traditionally made by male members of family
    B. Carved from tree roots
    C. Painted with clay and other natural pigments
        1. Significance of colors
        2. Meanings of various symbols used to decorate masks on dolls

Props and Audio-Visual Aids

There are all sorts of props and audio-visual aids you can use in a presentation. They include such things as drawings, photographs, charts, maps, diagrams, graphs, models, costumes, slides, films, records, tape recordings, and videotapes.

In many cases, your project itself serves as a prop or audio-visual aid. If you have built a model that shows the parts of the human brain, for example, it may be all you need in your presentation. But some projects benefit from the creation of additional props or visual aids. For example, if your project consists of doing a science experiment that would be difficult or impossible to reproduce during your presentation, you could prepare a series of drawings showing the different steps you followed in the experiment.

Props and audio-visual aids should always serve a definite purpose in your presentation.

Props and audio-visual aids should always serve a definite purpose in your presentation. Do not add them in a desperate attempt to improve a presentation that is short on facts. Fancy charts or a stack of photographs should never take the place of what you have to say in your presentation. And don't duplicate information in more than one visual aid. It makes little sense to point to a place on a globe if you are also displaying a map.

How Props and Aids Can Help

Props and audio-visual aids can play an important role in your presentation. If used properly, they can enhance your presentation by helping you meet your twin goals of conveying information clearly and keeping the audience interested in your presentation from start to finish.

Learning Aids. Some kinds of props and audio-visual aids make it easier for your audience to understand what you are talking about in your presentation. Models, charts, maps, and diagrams are examples of learning aids. In a presentation about how plants make food through photosynthesis, a series of diagrams can help the audience follow your explanation. If you are talking about the Battle of Bull Run during the Civil War, you might refer to a map that shows where the action took place.

Dramatizing a Point. Sometimes a prop or audio-visual aid can emphasize a point in a way that words alone can't do. For example, in a project that shows how cigarette smoking affects the lungs, a graph that compares the rate at which smokers and nonsmokers get lung cancer can be a powerful visual reinforcement for the message you are trying to get across in the presentation. Similarly, in a science presentation about the planet Jupiter, you can tell your audience that Jupiter's diameter is eleven times larger than that of the earth. But if you hold up a ping-pong ball to represent the earth, and a beach ball to represent Jupiter, your audience will probably be more impressed by the comparison.

Providing Examples. Many presentations can be made more effective if you use audio-visual aids as concrete examples of what you are talking about. For example, a discussion of Impressionist painting would probably be better if you showed the audience a number of prints of works by leading Impressionist artists. In a discussion of the uses of soybeans, you could display an array of products that contain soybeans in some form.

Setting a Mood. Some props and audio-visual aids enhance a presentation by helping to set an appropriate mood. In a dramatic reenactment of the landing of the *Mayflower,* for example, costumes and scenery can establish the setting. A travelog about Brazil could be presented with a tape of Brazilian music playing softly in the background.

Making Props and Audio-Visual Aids Effective

Remember that the whole point of including props and audio-visual aids is to improve your presentation by making it more understandable, more interesting, or more enjoyable for the audience. How can you be sure that your props or audio-visual aids will really be effective? Follow these guidelines:

1. Make sure your prop or audio-visual aid fits your purpose precisely. Think carefully about what information you want the prop or aid to convey, and then choose one that seems best suited to doing the job. If you are going to be talking about places where Maya Indian ruins have been located, don't choose a map of the entire world.

2. Don't use more props or audio-visual aids than you really need. You don't want to overpower the audience with a 'barrage of sights and sounds. Ideally, your presentation should be able to stand up on its own, and props and audio-visual aids should serve only to supplement what you say.

Don't use more props or audio-visual aids than you really need.

3. Make props and aids easy to understand. Don't clutter charts, graphs, diagrams, and other visual aids with a lot of unnecessary information. Label things clearly. Use bold lines and bright colors. The use of different colors in charts and graphs can make it easier for the audience to get the message these visual aids are meant to convey.

Make props and aids easy to understand.

4. Make visual aids big enough to be seen. It will not do much good to show a visual aid if people at the back or sides of the room cannot see it. Consider the size of your audience and the size of the room where you will be giving your presentation when you choose visual aids.

Ready-Made Props and Audio-Visual Aids

If you decide to include props or audio-visual aids in your presentation, you can turn to various sources to find appropriate material.

Look Around the House. Sometimes you can find just what you need right at home. The ping-pong ball and the beach ball used in the Jupiter presentation previously described are examples of the sorts of props or visual aids you might be able to find around the house.

Check Out the Library. The library is a good source to check for a variety of presentation tools. Many libraries have collections of art prints, photographs, films, slides, records, and tapes that can be checked out. They may also have equipment such as slide projectors and tape players that you can use.

Write to Outside Sources. Organizations that provide research information, such as government agencies, chambers of commerce, and professional associations, may also be able to provide visual aids. Many of these organizations publish posters, illustrated brochures, and other useful items.

Making Your Own Props and Aids

Sometimes the best props and audio-visual aids are the ones you prepare yourself. You can custom design them to include exactly the information you want. If you decide to make your own, be sure to allow enough time in your overall project schedule for the extra work involved. It is better to do a careful job preparing one or two props or audio-visual aids than to spread your effort among an assortment of creations.

Some of the most frequently used visual aids that you might make yourself are charts and graphs. There are various kinds of charts and graphs, and you should think carefully about which kind suits your purpose best.

Charts can present information in a variety of ways. The following list discusses some of the most useful kinds of charts:

Some of the most frequently used visual aids that you might make yourself are charts and graphs.

1. *Organization chart.* This kind of chart shows the chain of command of an organization. It can be used to show such things as the structure of the government of the Roman Empire or the structure of your local public utility commission.

2. *Classification chart.* Similar items are grouped together under various headings in a classification chart. For example, this is the kind of chart you would use if you wanted to put a list of minerals into two groups under the headings *Metallic Minerals* and *Nonmetallic Minerals.*

3. *Time line.* A time line gives the dates when a series of events took place. You can use time lines to show such things as the sequence of battles of the Civil War or highlights in the history of the development of computers.

4. *Table.* Statistics and other number information frequently appear in a table. You might use a table to show such things as the number of people who speak various languages in a country in Africa or for population statistics.

Classification Chart

PLANET TYPES

Terrestrial Planets   Major Planets

Mercury   Jupiter

Venus   Saturn

Earth   Uranus

Mars   Neptune

                   Unclassified

                      Pluto

Table

THE 10 LARGEST CITIES IN THE WORLD

Rank	City	Population
1.	Shanghai	11,859,748
2.	Mexico City	9,373,353
3.	Beijing (Peking)	9,230,687
4.	Seoul, South Korea	8,364,379
5.	Tokyo	8,349,209
6.	Moscow	8,275,000
7.	Bombay, India	8,227,332
8.	Tianjin, China	7,764,141
9.	New York City	7,164,742
10.	Sao Paulo, Brazil	7,033,529

Organization Chart

SAMPLE CORPORATE STRUCTURE

President

Vice President Sales / Vice President Marketing / Vice President Manufacturing

Eastern Sales Manager / Western Sales Manager

Manager Plant A / Manager Plant B

Time Line

THE 1820'S IN AMERICA

Missouri Compromise

James Monroe Becomes President

Monroe Doctrine

Erie Canal Completed

John Quincy Adams Becomes President

Democratic Party Formed

Tariff of Abominations

Andrew Jackson Becomes President

Indian Removal Act Passed

1820 1821 1822 1823 1824 1825 1826 1827 1828 1829 1830

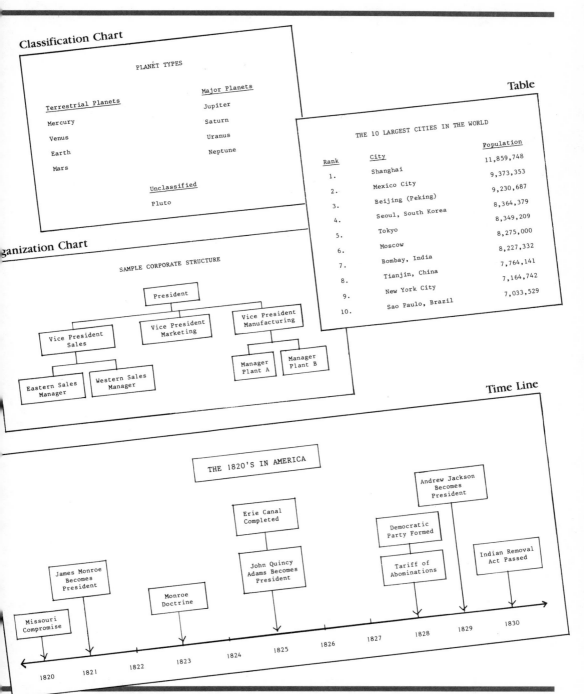

5. *Flow chart.* This kind of chart shows how a process operates or how material or information moves from a source to a destination. You could use a flow chart to show how soybeans are processed into margarine or to show the steps involved in transporting oil from Saudi Arabia to a gas station in the United States.

6. *Flip chart.* A flip chart is simply a series of charts clipped together at the top, so that the presenter can flip from one to another as a process or sequence of events is explained. It is far easier to use a flip chart than to try to shuffle through a series of separate charts during a presentation. To make a flip chart, begin by making the individual charts. Then make a summary chart that you can use during your conclusion. Put a plain cover on top of the charts, stack them in the correct order, and lay them on top of a slightly larger piece of plywood or heavy cardboard. Then staple the charts to the backing, or use rings to attach them. You can also use a large pad of newsprint or drawing paper as a ready-made blank flip chart.

Graphs are used to present number information in visual form so that it is clearer and easier for the audience to understand. The four most frequently used kinds of graphs are line graphs, bar graphs, circle graphs, and picture graphs:

1. Line graphs consist of vertical and horizontal base lines with numbers plotted at various points and connected with lines. Line graphs are frequently used to show an increase or decrease in number or quantity over a period of time. Population changes, for example, can be effectively portrayed in a line graph. By using different colors for lines representing different information, the audience can see at a glance how two sets of data compare. One line might represent population changes in an inner city, and another on the same graph might represent suburban population changes.

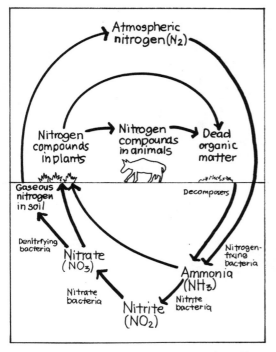

Flow Chart

Flip Chart

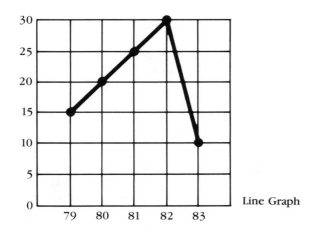

Line Graph

2. Bar graphs often can be used to portray the same sort of information as line graphs. Bar graphs can be horizontal or vertical.

3. Circle graphs show how the parts of something relate to the whole. They are often called pie charts, because they look like a pie with pieces of various sizes. Budget information is often presented in the form of pie charts that show how total income or expenses are divided among various categories. A simple pie chart for population figures might include one segment for rural population and one for urban population.

4. Picture graphs use picture symbols instead of lines, bars, or segments. Each symbol represents a specific quantity, and the reader can see at a glance how data compares. This is a simple form of graph that might be appropriate if you don't want to burden your audience with specific figures.

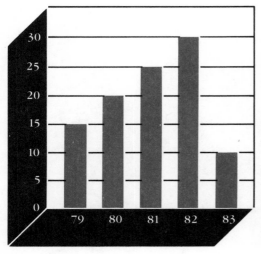

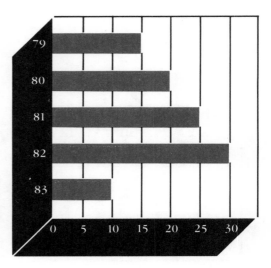

Bar Graphs

Group Projects

Group projects present special opportunities. If your group works together well, you can accomplish more together than you could individually, and your project can be more elaborate.

The key to successful group projects is cooperation—from start to finish. You need to plan carefully, carry through on your individual responsibilities, and practice your presentation together to assure a job well done.

Planning a Group Project

Simply choosing a project that every member of your group wants to do can be a challenge. Try to be flexible and come to an agreement that leaves everyone at least partly satisfied.

Once you have agreed on a project, divide up the responsibilities equally, so that no one member of the group is unfairly burdened. Also, take into consideration each person's talents and abilities, and use them to the best advantage of the group as a whole. For example, in a group

The key to successful group projects is cooperation—from start to finish.

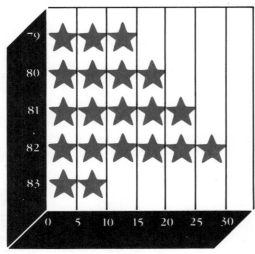

Picture Graph

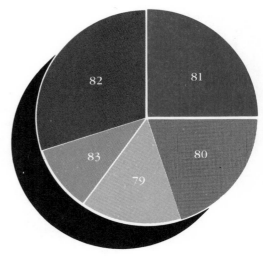

Circle Graph

project to reenact the adoption of the Declaration of Independence, one or two people might write the script, another person might make or gather props, and another could paint a backdrop. Be sure that each group member understands exactly what he or she is responsible for.

Your Responsibility to the Group

When you do a project on your own, the results reflect upon you as an individual. It is your time, talent, and diligence that show up in the end product. When you do a group project, your efforts may show up in only part of the end product, but you still need to do your best. Don't let down the other group members by sloughing off your responsibilities in the hopes that someone else will make up for your negligence. It is just not fair. Remember that a successful group project depends on the individual efforts of each participant.

Rehearsing for a Group Presentation

Remember that a successful group project depends on the individual efforts of each participant.

A group presentation of a project requires individual preparation followed by coordination among all of the group members. If each person practices his or her part of the presentation alone beforehand, rehearsing together will go more smoothly. Section III presents tips for rehearsing that you can use when you are practicing alone and with the group.

Without a doubt, it is easier to waste time when you are rehearsing with other people than when you are on your own. Resist the temptation to spend your rehearsal time talking about things that are not related to the project.

Keeping on Track

As you can see, there are many steps involved in producing a project and presenting it effectively. Use the following check list of questions to help keep yourself on track as you tackle a project assignment:

A Project and Presentation Check List

1. Have I chosen a project that reflects my interests?

2. Have I taken advantage of any background experience or knowledge that could be useful?

3. Have I checked to make sure that all necessary materials are available?

4. Do I have enough time to do a good job, or do I need to scale down my plans?

5. Will I be able to present my project within the time allotted for the presentation?

6. Have I analyzed my audience for such factors as age, education level, and familiarity with the topic?

7. Will my project and presentation be appropriate for the size of the audience?

8. Have I determined whether the purpose of my project is to inform, to persuade, or to entertain?

9. Have I done careful research, checking the best available sources?

10. Have I organized my presentation so that it has a logical format, with an attention-getting introduction, a supportive body, and an effective conclusion?

11. Have I considered what kinds of props or audio-visual aids might help make my presentation more effective?

12. Have I allowed enough time to make or find good props or audio-visual aids?

If you have completed all the steps involved in developing your project and presentation and can answer *yes* to all the above questions, you are ready to move on to the next phase, which is rehearsing your presentation.

III REHEARSING YOUR PRESENTATION

All phases of rehearsing your presentation, from proper speaking and delivery techniques to rehearsal tips with audio-visual aids, are presented in this section.

Choosing a Delivery Format   51

A Step-by-Step Approach
to Rehearsals   57

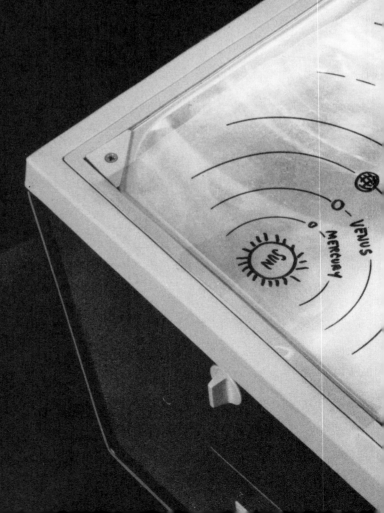

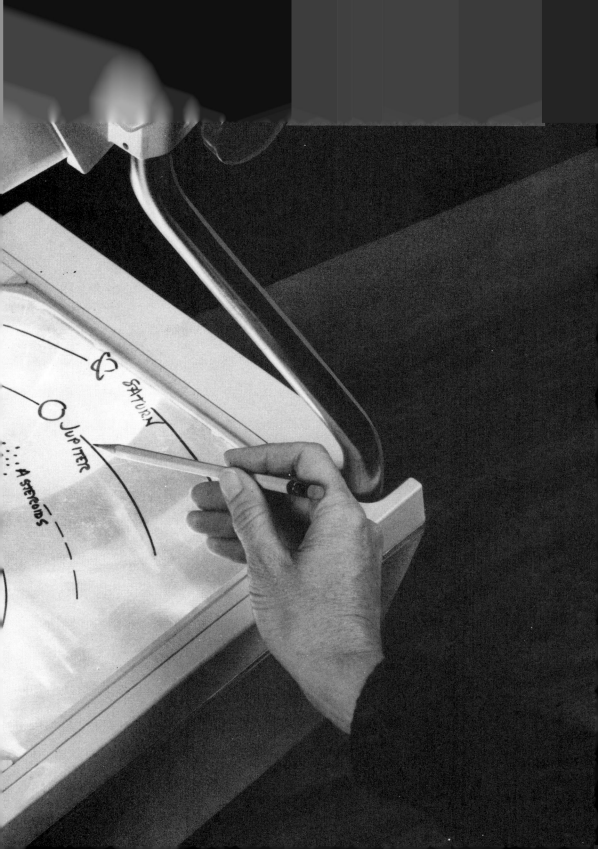

Rehearsing Your Presentation

W*hen your project is finally finished and the day comes for everyone to make presentations in front of the class, are you the one who raises your hand and volunteers to go first? Or do you slink down in your seat and hope the teacher will think you are not there?*

If you fall into the second category, you are not unusual. Most students enjoy doing their projects, but the presentation makes them feel at least a little uncomfortable. If your presentation is to be made to a group of adults or to the rest of the school, you might even feel terrified at the thought of giving your presentation.

One way to make the prospect of a presentation seem less frightening is to think of it as a conversation with the audience. If you are like most people, you have already had a lot of practice in carrying on a conversation. You probably spend several hours a day talking—with your family, your friends, your teachers, and countless other people you come into contact with day after day. You probably don't feel particularly nervous in these kinds of speaking situations. Yet, if you have to get up in front of your class or some other audience, you suddenly feel nervous. If you try to remember that your audience is simply a collection of individuals—just like the ones you speak to every day in other situations—you may feel more relaxed about getting up to speak.

The second way to overcome your feelings of nervousness and uncertainty is to follow the old Boy Scout motto: "Be Prepared." While you are working on your project and preparing your presentation, leave yourself plenty of time to rehearse. Rehearsing your presentation is the best way to gain the self-confidence you need in order to do a good job.

Choosing a Delivery Format

Before you actually begin to rehearse, you need to decide what format you will use for your presentation. You have three choices:

1. You can read from a manuscript.

2. You can memorize the presentation.

3. You can speak extemporaneously.

Each format has advantages and disadvantages. Some are better suited to certain kinds of projects than others. Let's take a closer look at each kind of delivery format and the rehearsal techniques that can help you use each one successfully.

Reading from a Manuscript

Reading from a manuscript is the format you would use if your project consisted of doing a dramatic reading—such as a short story, or a poem. But many students are tempted to use it for other presentations as well.

Pros and Cons

Reading from a manuscript may seem like the easy way out. You don't have to worry about forgetting anything, and if there is a time limit on the presentation, you can make sure that yours does not go on too long. Reading from a manuscript generally requires less time in actual rehearsal than the other formats, though you need to spend time writing out the complete text of your presentation if you are not just reading from a book.

Reading from a manuscript does have a number of disadvantages. Most of them relate to the fact that the written manuscript gives you little opportunity to develop a good relationship with your audience. When you are reading, it is easy to pay such close attention to the words on the page that you begin speaking in a monotone. You may forget to look up at the audience periodically, and the overall effect of your presentation could be dull and boring. If you keep your head down while reading, it may even be difficult for some people in the audience to hear you. This kind of delivery is likely to make the audience lose interest, and if that happens, the whole point of your presentation may never get across.

Reading from a manuscript also makes it difficult to change your presentation in response to audience reactions or unexpected situations that may occur. Because you are tied to your manuscript, you are not likely to insert additional information into your presentation if the audience seems particularly interested in one aspect of the topic.

Techniques for Good Reading

If you decide to read from a manuscript—or a book, for that matter—make a special effort to make your voice sound interesting by varying your pitch, your volume, and the rate at which you speak. Hold the manuscript up slightly rather than down on a table or desk top. This will make it easier for you to look up occasionally, and it will make your voice project outward toward the audience instead of down toward your papers. Be sure to practice reading your manuscript over and over again, so that you become thoroughly familiar with the material and can avoid having to read every word on the page. Eventually, you may find that you need to glance at the manuscript only occasionally, and you can establish the audience contact that helps make a presentation successful.

Preparing a Manuscript for Reading

When you prepare a manuscript that you are going to read for a presentation, you need to write it in a way that will sound natural when you are reading it aloud. You probably speak more informally than you write, and you want your presentation to convey that kind of natural, conversational tone.

Type or print your manuscript on one side of the paper, or use note cards.

Type or print your manuscript on one side of the paper, or use note cards. Number the papers or cards so that you can easily keep them in proper order. Underline

> It is important, of course, to
> recognize that the average citizen today
> is better educated and more knowledgeable
> than the average citizen of a generation
> ago-/-more literate, and exposed to more
> mathematics, literature, and science.//
> The positive impact of this fact on the

words that you want to stress. Mark pauses with vertical lines. You may want to use one line for a brief pause and two lines for a longer pause. Some speakers even make notes or symbols on their manuscript to indicate when they should look up at the audience. These various marks can help you overcome the danger of losing your audience's attention when you are reading from a manuscript.

Memorizing Your Presentation

Memorization is an appropriate choice if you are presenting a play or another sort of dramatization. But many students use it for any sort of presentation, especially if the teacher has specifically ruled out the option of reading from a manuscript.

Pros and Cons

Memorizing a presentation gives some students the confidence they need to get up before a group to speak. They like the security of knowing that every word they intend to say has been carefully rehearsed beforehand.

But beware. Memorizing a presentation has many drawbacks. In the first place, it can require hours or days of extra preparation time. Secondly, unless you consciously work on varying your tone of voice, a memorized presentation can sound stiff and unnatural. It is unlikely you can achieve the conversational approach you should be striving for in your presentation if you are concentrating on remembering the precise order of words you have memorized. Third, like reading from a manuscript, memorizing a presentation does not give you the flexibility to change your presentation according to audience reaction. Finally, if you experience a sudden memory block, your presentation could turn out to be a disaster.

Memory Tips

If you decide that memorizing your presentation is the best route to follow, there are a few tips that can help make your memorizing simpler. But don't expect the task of memorizing your presentation to be an easy one.

Abraham Lincoln used to read the newspaper aloud. When someone asked him why he did this, he supposedly replied, "When I read aloud, two senses catch the idea: first, I see what I read; second I hear it, and therefore can remember it better." You can use Lincoln's technique to help you memorize your presentation. Begin by typing or writing out a complete manuscript. Then read it over and over again, aloud and silently, so that you hear the words and see them on the page. Keep your paragraphs short, so that you can see them in your mind as distinct blocks.

Spread your rehearsal out over several sessions. Don't try to memorize your entire presentation at one time. Do it in small bits and pieces. Some speakers recommend that you begin by memorizing the first paragraph only. Once you have that down, go on and memorize the second paragraph. Then link the two together and recite them as one unit. Go on to memorize the third paragraph. When that one is firmly in mind, recite the first, second, and third paragraphs together. Continue in this manner until you have memorized the entire presentation. Then practice it in various places and under a variety of circumstances—on the way to school, in the shower, or before you go to sleep at night.

Don't try to memorize your entire presentation at one time. Do it in small bits and pieces.

Some people create mental pictures to help them memorize material. They visualize what they are talking about, and it helps them move from one idea to the next as they give their presentation. You can try this technique and see if it works for you.

Speaking Extemporaneously

Speaking extemporaneously means making up the exact words in your speech as you go along. Extemporaneous speaking involves careful advance work. You gather the facts you want to present and organize your material in an outline or on note cards. The outline or notes guide your presentation. In this sense, extemporaneous speaking differs from what is known as impromptu speaking, which is speaking with little or no preparation. Impromptu speaking is something you should avoid when you are giving a presentation.

Pros and Cons

Extemporaneous speaking is the best choice for most presentations. It is both organized and spontaneous. Your outline serves to keep you on track as you make your presentation, and it helps you remember all the important points you want to get across. Yet, because you haven't memorized every word, you can express yourself in a natural, conversational manner. It is easy to look at your audience and keep their attention. This format also gives you the flexibility to add or omit details based on audience reaction and interest.

Some students get nervous at the thought of relying on an outline or notes for their presentation. They are unsure of their ability to speak spontaneously in clear, complete sentences that follow one another in logical order, or they are afraid they might forget the details that are supposed to fill in the blanks between the outline headings.

The best cure for such fears is preparation. Gather more facts than you actually need for your presentation, and learn about the topic in depth. If you really know the information, you don't need to worry.

Preparing an Outline for Your Delivery

When you prepare an outline for delivery, don't make it so long and detailed that it looks like a manuscript. On the other hand, don't make it so brief and general that it really doesn't serve its purpose—which is to help you remember specifically what you want to say.

If you prepared an outline when you organized your presentation, you can use it as the basis of your delivery outline. Be sure to write out the first sentences of your introduction and your conclusion in full, though. This will prevent you from forgetting these crucial parts of your presentation. Some people also like to write out the first sentence of each paragraph as a way to guarantee that they will stay on track during their presentation. If you prefer, you can just use phrases for the rest of your outline. If your presentation includes statistics, include the exact figures in your outline. Underline key words or phrases, and add notations to show where you plan to refer to a visual aid or prop.

①

The pioneers

The story of the pioneers is a thrilling tale of men and women who pushed America's frontier from the Appalachian Mountains to the Pacific Ocean.

②

Moving westward

A. Crossing the Appalachians

B. How the pioneers traveled

③

A pioneer Settlement

A. A pioneer home (show model)

B. Education and Religion

C. Social activity

D. Indian attacks

You can write your outline on a single sheet of paper, or on note cards. Write on only one side of the paper or note cards. If you use cards, write just a few notes on each card, and make the words large enough so that you can read the notes easily. Be sure to number the cards in consecutive order.

Some people who speak extemporaneously write out a complete manuscript, then compose notes or an outline from it. This is the procedure that Winston Churchill followed whenever he prepared a speech. The danger in doing this, however, especially for an inexperienced speaker, is that you may be tempted to memorize the words you put down in the manuscript. If you do that, you lose all the advantages of the extemporaneous approach and take on all the burdens of the memorized delivery.

When you begin rehearsing an extemporaneous presentation, use your outline as your guide. Each time you rehearse, your presentation should sound a little bit different. You may phrase things differently or add a bit of information one time that you eliminate the next. Don't worry about these minor differences. They are exactly what make an extemporaneous presentation sound fresh and spontaneous when you deliver it.

Go through the complete presentation each time you rehearse. If you make a mistake or forget something, just keep going. Otherwise you end up with an overrehearsed introduction, and the rest of your presentation will not sound as polished. This method also prepares you for the possibility of something similar happening during your actual presentation. If you just keep going, your audience will probably never know the difference.

A Step-by-Step Approach to Rehearsals

When you rehearse a presentation, keep in mind that your audience will be judging your performance in two different areas. They will be listening to what you say, and they will also be looking at you. You need to rehearse both the vocal and the visual elements of your presentation.

If you take a step-by-step approach to your rehearsal, you can cover all the bases. Begin by rehearsing what you are going to say, using the various techniques previously described for each kind of delivery. Next, practice the visuals—gestures, facial expressions, and movements. Finally, put them together in a trial run before a preview audience of family or friends. You will find that this kind of careful approach to rehearsing will pay off in a smooth, self-confident presentation.

Judging the Content of Your Presentation

As you rehearse your presentation, try to listen critically to your sentences. Do they sound natural?

As you rehearse your presentation, try to listen critically to your sentences. Do they sound natural? You shouldn't use slang or incomplete sentences in your presentation, but you do want to strive for a conversational style. Be on the lookout for information gaps—places where you should add more details or explanatory material. Make sure that one point follows another in a logical order.

Analyzing Your Voice

The way your voice sounds can make a big difference in how effective your presentation will be. One of the best ways to analyze your voice is to make a tape recording of your presentation. Most people are surprised when they hear their voice on tape. The voice that others hear when you speak does not sound quite the same as your voice as you hear it.

There are a number of vocal elements to consider as you rehearse your presentation and listen to your tape. These include volume, speed, pitch, clarity of pronunciation, and energy level.

Volume

Volume refers to how loudly you speak. Obviously you want everyone in the audience to be able to hear you. You need to take into consideration such factors as the size of the audience, the size of the room, and whether or not there are outside noises you have to speak over. If you are making your presentation in the school auditorium, you may be using a microphone. If so, you can speak at about the same volume you would if you were in a face-to-face conversation.

Sometimes varying the volume of your voice can add an element of interest. You can speak loudly to emphasize a point or switch to a soft volume to gain the audience's attention and make them listen more carefully to a particular point. Don't overdo it, though. Unless you are giving a dramatic presentation, too many variations in volume can sound unnatural.

Speed

Many people speak too fast when they are giving a presentation because they are nervous. The words tumble out and are sometimes difficult to understand. Don't speak so quickly that you slur your words. If you have a time limit, try to keep up a steady pace so that you don't have to hurry at the end to get in the last bits of information. Sometimes, however, it can be effective to purposely vary the speed of your presentation. You can slow down to emphasize a point or use a dramatic pause after a particularly important statement. Again, be sure not to overdo such variations.

Pitch

Pitch refers to how high or low your voice sounds. Your speaking voice has an overall high or low pitch, but in normal conversation you vary the pitch automatically to a certain extent. Your voice may sound higher when you are excited and lower when you are serious. When you are making a presentation, strive to maintain a normal variation in pitch, and avoid speaking in a monotone.

Clarity of Pronunciation

Whenever you make a presentation, it is important to pronounce every word clearly and correctly so that the audience knows exactly what you are talking about. This is especially important if you are explaining something that might be new to the audience or using technical or otherwise unfamiliar words. If you find that you consistently stumble over a particular word, use a different one. Take care to pronounce the final consonants of words and final endings, such as *-ing* and *-ed*.

Energy Level

When you chose your project, you hopefully selected something that you found interesting to do. Your enthusiasm should be an asset now, when you are preparing your presentation. If you are enthusiastic about your topic, your audience is more likely to be interested in what you have to say. Your voice conveys that sense of enthusiasm through its energy level. A delivery that is flat and boring will put the audience to sleep even if the information contained in the presentation is interesting. On the other hand, an enthusiastic speaker can make an audience pay attention even if the material is not very exciting.

If you are enthusiastic about your topic, your audience is more likely to be interested in what you have to say.

Sloppy Speech Habits

Avoid saying "uh" and "er" between words and phrases. Just pause instead. No one will mind. If you have a habit of saying "like, uh," "you know," "well, um," and similar meaningless phrases, work to eliminate them from your presentation.

Checking Your Body Language

The term *body language* refers to the way you use your body to communicate. Such things as posture, facial expressions, eye contact, and gestures are elements of body language.

Probably the best way to analyze your body language is to make a videotape of yourself during one of your rehearsals. Watching yourself on the screen is the next best thing to sitting in the audience on presentation day. If you don't have videotape equipment available, however, rehearsing in front of a mirror can be very helpful.

Posture

When you rehearse and later when you give your presentation, stand up straight but not rigid. If you are too stiff, your audience will sense that you are nervous. But if you slouch, you may appear bored or tired, and your voice will not sound its best. Your posture should convey a sense of confidence and enthusiasm.

Facial Expressions

When you are having an everyday conversation with someone, you generally change your facial expression in many ways. You smile, frown, raise your eyebrows, and otherwise react to what you are saying and hearing. When you give a presentation, your face should reflect the same sorts of reactions. As you rehearse, notice how your face changes as you speak. Don't purposely add grins or grimaces that look overdone or unnatural, but strive to keep your face looking expressive, rather than blank.

Eye Contact

Keeping in touch with your audience by looking at them is an important way to keep their attention. If you look at the ceiling or the floor while you are making your presentation, you will appear distracted, and the audience may soon also be distracted. Remember that you want your presentation to appear as relaxed and natural as a conversation. It is considered rude to look away from a person when you are having a conversation. If you don't maintain eye contact with your audience during your presentation, they might think you are not really interested in talking to them.

When rehearsing, practice looking at different objects in the room as you speak. When you are actually giving your presentation, try to keep your eyes moving from the center to the sides of the audience rather than looking at just one person. Look at people's faces, not over their heads.

Keeping in touch with your audience by looking at them is an important way to keep their attention.

Gestures

Gestures can be an important element in your presentation if they are used appropriately. You can gesture with your hands, your arms, and your head. You can use gestures to add emphasis to an important point and to move from one point to the next. Be careful not to overdo gestures, though. If you gesture constantly, your gestures will lose their effect, and the audience will begin to pay more attention to your movements than to your words. Only use gestures that you are comfortable with and that appear to blend in naturally with what you are saying.

Rehearsing with Props and Audio-Visual Aids

If your presentation includes props and audio-visual aids, you should rehearse with these items so that you can incorporate them smoothly into your talk. An otherwise fine presentation could be ruined if you have to struggle with a poorly constructed chart or if you find at the last moment that you don't know how to operate the slide projector that you had planned to use. Use the following list of suggestions to guide your rehearsal and help assure effective use of props and audio-visual aids during your presentation:

1. Mount illustrations (charts, diagrams, and maps) and set them up on an easel rather than trying to hold them while speaking.

2. If you are going to write on a chalkboard or paper, remember to keep turning back to your listeners to maintain your eye contact with them and to keep your voice projecting out toward the audience. If possible, write or draw without speaking, then turn and face the audience and resume where you left off.

3. Don't pass a visual aid or prop around to your audience during your presentation. It's too distracting. Wait until you have finished, and then pass the material around.

4. Don't stand in front of a prop or visual aid, or otherwise block the view of any part of your audience. Use a pointer, rather than your hand, when referring to a chart, map, or similar visual aid.

5. Remember to talk to the audience, not to the prop or visual aid.

Tips for Using Audio-Visual Equipment

If you will be using such equipment as a video recorder, tape recorder, or slide projector, rehearse with it so that you are thoroughly familiar with how it operates. Make certain the equipment is in good working order and that an electrical outlet is nearby in your classroom or any other presentation site.

Using a Slide Projector

You can use a slide projector to show your own original slides or purchased slides. If possible, use a projector with a remote control device, so that you can remain at the front of the room while describing the slides.

Take the time to arrange your slides carefully in proper sequence. Make sure the slides are all facing the right way so that you are not embarrassed by slides that appear on the screen backwards or upside down. Put a mark on each slide to indicate its proper position in the slide tray. You will probably have to darken the room when you are presenting your slides, so be sure you have a flashlight or some other means to see your notes.

Using an Opaque Projector

An opaque projector enlarges two-dimensional objects that are too small to be seen by your audience—such as a coin, a leaf, or a stamp—and projects the image on a screen. It can be helpful if you want to show a map, a chart, or other materials from a book without having to make a special slide or transparency. You can also use it to project an image of a three-dimensional object of a certain size.

An opaque projector should only be used for audiences of classroom size or smaller. You need to darken the room completely so that the image can be seen, so remember to bring a flashlight to read your notes. Be careful not to let the projector get overheated. The projector's lamp may get so hot that some parts of the projector cannot be touched, and it may even damage what you are projecting.

Using an Overhead Projector

An overhead projector passes light through a transparency and projects the image through a lens and mirror system and then over the shoulder of the operator onto a screen. This means that you can face your audience as you operate the projector—an obvious advantage for maintaining contact. In addition, it can usually be used in a lighted room.

The transparency is a sheet of clear plastic that can be imprinted with an image. You can buy transparencies ready-made or make them yourself. To make a transparency, you can simply write or draw on the sheet of plastic with special marking pens. You can also make one by running a frosted sheet of acetate through a ditto machine. You can also use a copying machine and specially treated film to make a transparency.

You can create transparencies during your presentation by drawing or writing on them as your speak. You can add details to transparencies you made earlier or highlight features you want to emphasize. You can also lay one transparency over another to build up a complex picture from a series of simple ones.

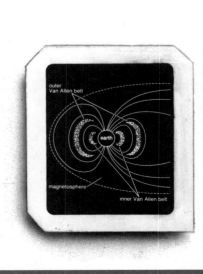

Using a Filmstrip Projector

A filmstrip projector displays the images on a roll of film, one frame at a time. There are usually from twenty to sixty images on a roll. You can use a ready-made filmstrip or have one made from your own slides. The sequence of images on a filmstrip cannot be changed. If you only want to show certain images, you still need to move through the roll to get to the ones you want. Also, you need to darken the room to show a filmstrip.

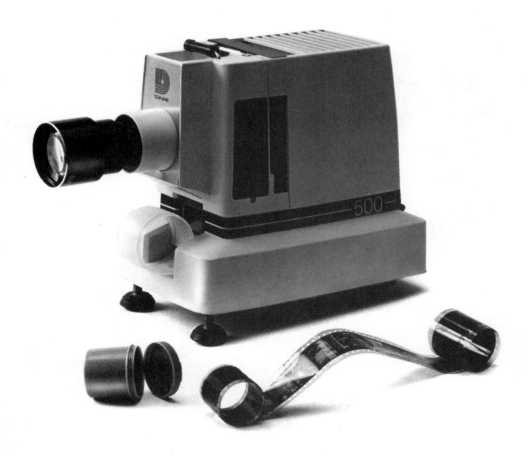

Using a Videotape Player

A videotape player shows videotapes on a television screen. You need to be sure the screen is large enough so that the entire audience can see the tape. Depending on the features of the recorder, you may be able to freeze a frame on the screen or create special effects by operating the tape in slow motion or fast forward.

Using a Tape Recorder

A tape recorder can be used to play music or speech—either your own original work or someone else's. If you are using a small portable tape recorder, make sure the volume will be loud enough so that everyone can hear clearly. You may need to plug the recorder into a set of auxiliary speakers if you will be using it in a large room. If you do use speakers, be sure they are facing the audience and are not obstructed by a desk, podium, plant, or some other object. Keep the tape recorder next to you so that you can turn it on and off at precisely the right moment.

Using a Record Player

A record player requires careful operation to make sure you put the needle down at just the right place on the record. Otherwise, your audience will be distracted as they hear fragments of sounds that are not part of your presentation. If you have a choice between a tape recorder and a record player, use a tape recorder.

Presenting a Trial Run

After you have rehearsed several times on your own, you may feel confident enough to go right ahead with your presentation. But sometimes it is hard to judge your own work and performance. Before you make your actual presentation, it is a good idea to ask a family member or friend to act as a preview audience. A trial run of this sort gives you a chance to make changes and polish your performance even more, so that the actual presentation will be as good as it can be.

Ask your preview audience to be objective and honest in judging your presentation. They may be able to note gaps in content or problems in pronunciation and other vocal elements. They may notice distracting mannerisms that you are not even aware of, such as twisting your hair or rocking from one foot to the other.

Ask for suggestions on how to improve your performance, and do what you can to correct any defects that may be pointed out. Don't be upset if the trial run doesn't get rave reviews. After all, you are still in the rehearsal stage. If you can repeat the trial run after you've had a chance to work on your presentation some more, the feedback should be much more positive the second time around, adding to your self-confidence as presentation day approaches.

Visiting the Presentation Site

For most school projects, your presentation will occur in a very familiar place—your classroom. You hardly need to make a special visit to the classroom to check out its size or acoustics. But you should check such things as the location of electrical outlets if you need to plug in a projector or other piece of equipment. You might have to bring along an extension cord if your equipment cord will not reach a nearby outlet. If you are going to be showing slides or a movie, check to make sure a screen is available and curtains can be shut so the room will be dark enough.

If your presentation site is somewhere other than your classroom, it becomes even more important to visit it beforehand and check on what is available. Perhaps you will be speaking from the stage in the school auditorium or in the gymnasium. You will need to project your voice much more in a large space than would be necessary in a classroom.

If possible, rehearse your presentation at the site. Ask a friend to come along and tell you if your voice can be heard and your props or visual aids can be easily seen.

If you will be using a podium and a microphone, try rehearsing with them, also, so that you don't get flustered by having to deal with something unfamiliar on the day of your presentation. Learn how to turn the microphone on and off and how to adjust it up and down, so that it will be at the right height for your presentation. Determine how far away from the microphone you should stand to get the best effect.

A Final Review

Depending on how complicated your project and presentation are, rehearsals may take a lot of time. But they will help you go from uncertainty to self-confidence. As a final assurance before your actual presentation, go through the following list of questions to make sure your rehearsals have covered everything:

A Rehearsal Check List

1. Have I chosen a delivery that is appropriate for my project and that I feel comfortable with?

2. Have I prepared a manuscript, outline, or note cards to guide my presentation?

3. Have I rehearsed enough times so that I don't have to read every word on my manuscript or notes?

4. Have I judged the content of my presentation to make sure all necessary information is included and the audience will be able to follow every point?

5. Have I timed my presentation so that it fits within the required time limit, if any?

6. Have I analyzed my voice for such elements as volume and speed, and tried varying my volume and speed for added effectiveness?

7. Have I been careful to avoid speaking in a monotone?

8. Am I sure of the pronunciation of every word in my presentation, and am I careful to pronounce endings clearly?

9. Have I eliminated sloppy speech habits from my presentation?

10. Do I sound enthusiastic about my topic?

11. Is my posture erect, but relaxed?

12. Does my facial expression look pleasant and natural?

13. Have I practiced looking at various objects as I speak, so that I will have good eye contact with the audience during my presentation?

14. Are my speaking gestures appropriate and natural looking?

15. Do I know precisely when I will refer to a visual aid?

16. Have I practiced with my visual aids so that I am comfortable using them?

17. Have I remembered to speak toward the audience instead of to the visual aid?

18. Have I practiced using audio-visual equipment so I am thoroughly familiar with how it works?

19. Am I thoroughly familiar with the presentation site and its facilities?

If you can answer *yes* to all of these questions, you are ready to go ahead with your presentation. You can proceed knowing that you have done everything possible to ensure a successful outcome. Good luck!

IV MAKING YOUR PRESENTATION

This section tells you how to carry out your actual presentation, with special tips on how to handle stage fright, audience reactions, and unexpected problems.

Setting Up	80
Your Personal Appearance	80
Stage Fright	81
Judging Audience Reaction	84
Question-and-Answer Sessions	85
Unexpected Problems	87

Making Your Presentation

Y ou worked hard to create a successful project, and you rehearsed your presentation thoroughly. Now, finally, the day has arrived to make your presentation. This is the time when you share what you learned with your audience.

Setting Up

During your rehearsals, you should have checked any equipment you planned to use to make sure it is in good working order. On the day of the presentation, you should double-check everything. If your props or visual aids use batteries, bring fresh ones. If you are using a slide or movie projector, bring along a spare light bulb.

Sometimes it is a good idea to keep props or visual aids handy, but hidden, until you are ready to use them. This is particularly true if your visual aid is unusual. If it is in plain view before your presentation, the audience may be so distracted that they don't pay attention to your introductory remarks. If your props or visual aids need to be assembled, do as much as possible before you are scheduled to begin, so that you don't waste time and cause the audience to grow impatient.

Your Personal Appearance

It is important to project a positive self-image when you give your presentation. You want to look neat and clean. Unless you are wearing a costume for your presentation, dress in simple, comfortable clothes. If you will be pointing to a visual aid or otherwise gesturing, make sure that you can do so without buttons popping or seams tearing. Remember that you want your listeners to pay attention to what you have to say, not to what you are wearing. Avoid unusual jewelry or clothing that might distract the audience. Don't wear an armful of jangling bracelets, for example, that will clatter every time you make a gesture.

Stage Fright

No matter how well prepared you are, you will probably experience some feelings of nervousness before your turn to make your presentation. Even the friends and classmates that you talk with almost every day may suddenly take on a whole new dimension when you are standing in front of them and their faces are all turned toward you expectantly. If you are speaking before a group of parents or any large or unfamiliar gathering, your tension may be even greater.

The Symptoms

Stage fright is a reaction to a stressful situation. It is generally based on a fear of not performing well or of making a mistake. Not everyone reacts in exactly the same way, but there are a number of common symptoms that people experience when they are afraid. When you are feeling the effects of stage fright, your body and mind may react in various ways, both physical and mental.

Physical Symptoms

A feeling of "butterflies in your stomach" is a common sign of stage fright. You may notice your heart beating a little faster than usual, and you may find yourself slightly short of breath. Your mouth may feel dry, and your voice may sound higher than usual. Sweaty palms are another common symptom. You may notice that your underarms are also perspiring more than usual, or that your face feels warm. Your knees, hands, or voice may tremble. You may find yourself swallowing repeatedly or licking your lips.

A feeling of "butterflies in your stomach" is a common sign of stage fright.

Mental Symptoms

Before you begin to speak, you may find yourself thinking such thoughts as "I don't want to do this! I should have prepared more! What if I forget something?" Your thoughts may become so confused and agitated that you actually fumble when you begin to speak. You may mispronounce words or make slips of the tongue. You may find yourself saying "uh" and "er" between sentences, as you try to remember what you planned to say next.

Keep in mind that few people experience all of these symptoms, and many people may have only one or two. Don't waste time beforehand worrying about how you may react.

Stage Fright Is Normal

You may be able to take some comfort in knowing that your feelings of anxiety are perfectly normal.

You may be able to take some comfort in knowing that your feelings of anxiety are perfectly normal. Two thousand years ago, the Roman orator Cicero said, "The better qualified the man is to speak, the more he fears the difficulty of speaking."

Today, professional actors and public speakers from presidents on down experience nervousness before they have to speak. Many professionals go so far as to say that a little bit of stage fright is good for you, because it makes you try harder. It is true that nervousness gives your body extra energy, and that energy can be used to make your performance more dynamic and stimulating. Just as many athletes perform at peak levels when they are keyed up before the race or game, many speakers also do their best when they are energized with a healthy bit of stage fright.

Keeping Stage Fright Under Control

Although stage fright is a normal reaction, it is important that you work on keeping it under control. A little bit is all right, but too much can ruin your presentation. You can fight back against the symptoms of stage fright with a variety of mental and physical strategies.

Mental Strategies

Replace the negative thoughts you may be having with positive thoughts. Use the following list of suggestions as your guide to achieving a more relaxed state of mind before your presentation:

1. Tell yourself that you are well prepared. Here is where all those hours of research, organizing, and rehearsing really pay off. If you have done a good job of preparing for your presentation, you really should have no major difficulties.

2. Put things in proper perspective. Keep in mind that your presentation is probably not going to change your life in any significant way. If something does go wrong, your friends are not going to abandon you, you will not be thrown out of school, and your parents will not ask you to leave home.

3. Listen to the person before you. Take your mind off your own presentation by paying close attention to the speakers who are giving their presentations before you. You should be giving them your full attention anyway, just as a matter of courtesy. But by making a real effort to pay attention to what others are saying, you push away negative thoughts that might otherwise crowd your brain.

4. Remind yourself that you are not alone. Most likely, you are not the only one who is making a presentation. Everyone else is probably experiencing some anxiety, also.

5. The audience is on your side. Most audiences want a speaker to do well. If anything goes wrong, they will probably be sympathetic.

6. Appearance counts. Most likely, you look far more confident than you feel inside. No one can see a churning stomach.

Physical Strategies

There are certain physical exercises you can do to lessen your tension. It might not be appropriate to do all of them in school, so you may want to do them at home on the morning of your presentation. But perhaps you can find a relatively private corner or other area where you will not be noticed. You should not do anything that will distract the speaker who is giving a presentation before yours. Try these exercises to lessen your tension:

1. Breathe deeply. Slow, deep breathing will actually slow your heart rate and help calm you down. Breathe through your nose, so that your mouth does not get dry.

2. Drop your head forward, and roll it slowly around in a circle from left to right, then from right to left.

3. Yawn several times to relax your face muscles.

4. Hold your arms out and slowly rotate them. Drop your hands to your sides and shake them vigorously to get rid of excess energy.

Get Up and Go

Your feelings of nervousness will probably decrease as soon as the words begin to come out of your mouth.

When the time comes for your presentation, take a deep breath and walk briskly to your place in front of the audience. Act confident, even if you don't feel 100 per cent confident. Most likely, your audience will not know the difference. If you need to set up equipment or audio-visual aids and props, do so before you begin to speak. Then look directly at your listeners to gain their attention, and begin. Your feelings of nervousness will probably decrease as soon as the words begin to come out of your mouth.

Judging Audience Reaction

Even if you rehearsed a hundred times, there is no way to know beforehand precisely how your audience will react to your presentation. So it is important to pay attention to your audience while you are speaking to take note of any feedback they may be giving you.

Feedback can come in two forms: audible and visible. Audible feedback includes such things as laughter or exclamations of surprise. Visible feedback includes things you can see—facial expressions, for example.

Audience reactions can also be classified as either positive feedback or negative feedback. If you are getting positive feedback—alert faces, expressions of interest, and so on—you know you are on the right track. You can proceed with your presentation with the added boost of assurance that comes from seeing your audience react favorably.

If you are getting negative feedback, don't panic. You may simply need to make some midcourse corrections. For example, if you notice people looking puzzled or confused, you may need to provide more explanatory details. If you see people at the back of the room straining to hear, you obviously need to speak up. You may notice people staring out the window or otherwise looking distracted. In that case, you may need to liven up your presentation. Perhaps you have fallen into a monotone and need to vary your pitch and boost your energy level. Maybe you should speed things up a bit.

Remember that your presentation should be like a conversation—but with many people instead of just one or two. When you talk with a friend, you probably adjust the way you speak according to your friend's reaction without even thinking about it. In a presentation, you need to make the same sort of adjustments. Don't put up a wall between yourself and the audience. Use their reactions to keep yourself energized or to improve your presentation as necessary. At the same time, don't let the reaction of just one or two people prompt major changes. If almost everyone in your audience seems interested, but one person is staring off into space, you are probably doing fine.

Question-and-Answer Sessions

When you give a presentation, your audience may have questions afterward. Sometimes this occurs because you didn't explain things adequately or because you left out facts that would have made your presentation clearer. Ideally, situations like this should be corrected during your rehearsal in front of your trial audience.

But questions are not necessarily a sign of a poor presentation. In fact, they may be a positive indicator—a sign that the audience was interested enough to pay close attention to what you said and would like to know more.

It is important to be prepared for the possibility of questions.

It is important to be prepared for the possibility of questions. Once again, here is where your research pays off. The information that you found but didn't include in the final presentation may come in handy when someone asks a question. You can prepare for possible questions during your trial run by having your preview audience ask a few. The experience will help you learn to think on your feet.

Here are some tips for conducting a successful question-and-answer session:

1. Be polite. You should handle questions with poise and politeness. Even if someone asks a silly question, do your best to be tactful and answer in a straightforward manner.

2. Be brief. Give the questioner the necessary information, but keep your answers brief. Don't launch into a whole new presentation on the basis of one question. It is unfair to the rest of the audience to tie up a lot of time with one response. If a questioner persists in asking a lot of follow-up questions, you can suggest that he or she consult one of your sources for more information.

3. Do not be afraid to say you don't know the answer to a question. No one expects you to be the world's greatest expert on your topic. It is far better to admit to not knowing the answer than to pass along incorrect information. Again, you can suggest that the questioner consult one of your sources for the answer, or you can offer to find out the information yourself and report back to the questioner at a later time.

Unexpected Problems

Sometimes, things go wrong with a presentation even if you prepared thoroughly and rehearsed repeatedly. You may trip on the way up to the front of the room. Someone in the audience may become sick. A sudden thunderstorm may cause an incredible sound-and-light show outside the window behind you. Although you should not dwell on the possibility of a foul-up, it is wise to think ahead about how you would handle various situations.

Trouble with Yourself

A number of different things can go wrong with you while speaking, and there is no way to anticipate all of them. Just remember that the key to handling such situations is to stay cool and maintain your concentration. Don't allow yourself to get flustered. If possible, ignore the situation and keep right on speaking. In many cases the audience will never know that something is amiss. If you cannot ignore a mishap, at least try to handle it with grace and good humor. Remind yourself that it is not the end of the world. Although you may be momentarily embarrassed, chances are people will not still be talking about your mishap a year later. And remember that it is highly unlikely that a mishap will ruin your entire presentation. Just do your best to keep on going.

If you drop your note cards, for example, gather them up quickly, arrange them in proper order, and proceed from where you left off. If you sneeze or cough, simply say, "Excuse me," and continue. If you become truly incapacitated, excuse yourself from the room to get a drink of water and then return and continue. Sometimes you mispronounce a word or say the wrong word and are not even aware of the mistake until the audience breaks out in laughter. When that happens, you can simply apologize and repeat your last sentence correctly. Or try handling the situation with good humor by saying something like "Pardon me while I untie my tongue" or "Let me try that one more time."

Trouble with the Audience

Sometimes, your listeners can cause problems during your presentation. We have already talked about paying attention to your audience and acting upon any negative feedback you may get from them. But other problems can also occur. If someone is making distractive movements or sounds, do your best to ignore these distractions. If it is not possible, you can pause briefly and ask the person to please stop. Then proceed.

Audience problems, like speaker problems, should not disrupt your entire presentation. Once again, the key to overcoming them is to maintain your poise and proceed as best you can.

Troubles with the Setting or Equipment

Your filmstrip breaks. A construction crew begins operating a jackhammer outside the open window. The lights go off. The overhead projector breaks down. All sorts of things can go wrong with your setting or equipment, in spite of your best efforts to check everything out beforehand.

If you know that a problem will be temporary—such as a loud jet passing overhead—just wait and then go on when the situation has improved. If the problem is uncorrectable, you can ask your teacher if it would be all right to reschedule your presentation. If that is not possible, you will just have to do the best you can under the circumstances. Again, your research may pay off handsomely if you run into a dilemma with your setting or equipment. You can tell the audience what they would have seen, had your filmstrip not broken. Perhaps you can draw on the chalkboard the diagrams that you had planned to show with the overhead projector. You may be able to fill in the gaps with additional information that you did not include in your rehearsed presentation.

Your research may pay off handsomely if you run into a dilemma with your setting or equipment.

Four Rules to Remember

Whatever the mishap—with yourself, with the audience, with the setting, or with the equipment—remember these four rules:

1. Stay calm.
2. Keep the situation under control.
3. Think quickly.
4. Proceed.

In almost all cases, you will be able to continue without any further problems. Do your best to put the mishap behind you so that the rest of your presentation will be the best that it can be.

This section contains more than 100 ideas for school projects.

Project Ideas for Social Studies   93

Project Ideas for Science   101

Project Ideas for Language Arts   105

Project Ideas for Math   108

Ideas for School Projects

I deas for school projects can come from many sources. Your textbooks and other required reading may have ideas for projects you can do on your own time. Browsing through encyclopedia articles in the subject area you are interested in can give you ideas. Sometimes a newspaper or magazine article will catch your eye and give you the information you need for the beginning of a project. Your library may have many books that are packed with suggestions for science experiments, arts and crafts projects, and hobby activities that can be adapted for a school project.

The rest of this section consists of more than 100 ideas for school projects. The ideas are grouped into four general subject headings: social studies, science, language arts, and math. Subheadings within each section lead you to more specific topics. For example, under the "Social Studies" heading, you find a subheading for "American History" with several related project ideas.

The list does not offer a complete rundown of project possibilities. It is merely a sampler. Its purpose is to help you discover some of the many different ways you can approach a project assignment. Use it as a spur to your own imagination and creativity. You may find an idea in this list that suits your needs exactly. Other ideas can be adapted to your particular topic.

Some of the ideas involve more work than others. You may be able to simplify a complicated project that appeals to you but that you don't have enough time to do. On the other hand, you may choose a relatively simple idea and use it as part of a more complicated project. The list includes a number of suggestions for group projects, as well as for projects to do on your own.

Project Ideas for Social Studies

Local Government

- (Group Project) **Government Debate**—Determine the type of government your city or town has. Organize a debate to discuss the pros and cons of this type of government compared to other types of local government.

State History, Geography, and Economics

- **State Wax Museums**—Use clay or some other modeling medium to create a miniature wax museum of famous people who were born in your state or who were important figures in its history.

- **State Diorama**—Create a diorama of paper or cardboard figures showing a famous event that took place in your state.

- **State Relief Map**—Use papier-mâché or clay to make a relief map of your state, including all major physical features.

- **State Economy Map**—Draw a map of your state, including major cities and towns. Use doll house miniatures, actual samples, or other devices to represent major agricultural and industrial products of your state, and glue them to the map in the appropriate locations.

American Indians

- **Historic Sites Indian Map**—Create a map of the United States showing the locations of historic sites or other places of interest having to do with American Indians.

- **Pueblo Village**—Make a clay model of an adobe village typical of the Pueblo Indians.

- **Navajo Weaving**—Use natural plant materials to dye yarn, then weave a swatch of cloth with a pattern inspired by a traditional Navajo design.

- **Navajo Sand Painting**—Create a traditional Navajo sand painting. Preserve it under glass or a piece of clear plastic. Explain the significance of such painting among the Navajo.

- **Hopi Kachina Dolls**—Make a Hopi Indian kachina doll and explain its meaning.

Eskimos

- **Snowhouse Models**—Construct models of a traditional Eskimo snowhouse, using sugar cubes or some other appropriate material, and a more modern dwelling that today's Eskimos might live in.

- **Eskimo Songs and Stories**—Select an Eskimo song or legendary story and tell it aloud. Then explain its significance as part of the Eskimo culture.

- **Soapstone Sculpture**—Carve an animal or Eskimo figure out of a large bar of soap, following the style of traditional Eskimo soapstone sculptors.

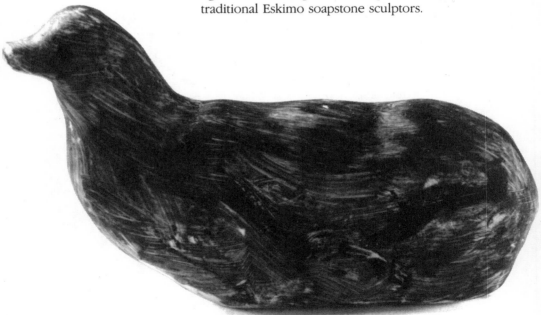

American History

- (Group Project) **Meet the Press, Christopher Columbus**—Present a dramatization, using the format of a television interview show, with special guest Christopher Columbus (in appropriate costume) questioned by three reporters about his voyages and discoveries.

- **New World Board Game**—Create a board game using the theme of travel to and settlement in the New World by early American colonists. The object of the game is to reach America safely and establish a successful settlement.

- (Group Project) **Colonial Justice**—Present a brief play depicting an incident in which a colonist is apprehended, tried, and punished for a minor offense. Make a model of a ducking stool, pillory, or stocks to use as a prop.

- **Revolutionary War Time Line**—Select one or more subject areas—such as science, music, literature—and create a time line that shows the achievements in those areas during the American Revolutionary War period of the 1770's and 1780's. As an alternative, select a foreign country or a continent, and make a time line that shows major events that took place there during the American Revolution.

- **Colonial Newscast**—Dress in appropriate colonial costume, and present a live or videotaped newscast describing the Boston Tea Party or another event in the Revolutionary War period. This can also be done as a group project if you include an enactment of the event you are covering.

- **Log Cabin Model**—Build a model of a pioneer log cabin, and describe the steps necessary to build this type of dwelling.

- (Group Project) **Class Convention**—Present a dramatization of a constitutional convention in which you draw up a constitution and bill of rights to govern your class.

- **Westward Movement Board Game**—Create a board game using the theme of the Westward Movement in the United States and incorporating the various dangers and rewards associated with the migration.

- **Revolutionary War Cartoons**—Create a series of political cartoons based on events leading up to the American Revolution.

- (Group Project) **King George Interview**—Interview King George III about his policies regarding the American Colonies in the 1760's and 1770's. Dress in appropriate costume for the role of interviewer and subject.

- (Group Project) **Women's Rights Newsreel**—Create a black-and-white newsreel depicting a women's rights rally or parade of the early 1900's. All participants should dress according to the styles of the times.

- **Depression Game**—Create a board game based on the theme of surviving the Great Depression. Players must overcome various economic catastrophes and mishaps to reach the goal of financial security.

- (Group Project) **Political Campaigns**—Create a modern media campaign for Theodore Roosevelt, Woodrow Wilson, or another presidential candidate of the early 1900's. Include some or all or the following: TV ads, radio ads, newspaper ads, news releases, campaign posters, and campaign buttons.

- **Recruiting Posters**—Draw an original design for a World War II armed forces recruiting poster.

- **Ethnic Map of the United States**—Devise a map of the United States that shows the nation's major ethnic groups and where they have settled. Use color-coded pins or some other device to indicate settlement patterns.

Ancient Civilizations

- **Hieroglyphics Pottery**—Make a vase or bowl out of clay, and decorate it with hieroglyphics and pictures or designs in the style of ancient Egypt.

- **Greek Clothing**—Sew a complete costume of classical Greek clothing. Model the costume and tell the correct name of each article.

- **Roman Mosaics**—Using colored tiles or bits of paper, make a mosaic depicting a scene from everyday life in ancient Rome or a scene from a Roman myth.

Map and Globe Skills

- **Meridian Travels**—On a map or globe, trace up and down the meridian closest to your hometown, and locate other cities and towns to the north and south that are on or close to the same meridian. Present a report about some of the towns, telling how they are similar to and/or different from your hometown. Accompany your presentation with a map or globe that shows the locations of the cities you discuss.

- **Sister City Search**—Make a model globe of the world. Pinpoint the precise location of your hometown, using the correct latitude and longitude. Then pinpoint the place on the globe that is at the same latitude, but 180° away in longitude. Locate a city or town at or near that location and tell about it, citing similarities and differences compared to your hometown.

Technology and Inventions

- **Transportation Time Line**—Create an illustrated time line of transportation inventions.

- **Printing History**—Carve a set of printing blocks out of wood or firm vegetables (such as potatoes or carrots), and print a page of text with them. Use them as a display for a presentation on the impact of the discovery of movable type.

- (Group Project) **Thomas Edison Interview**—Conduct an in-depth interview with Thomas Edison in his lab. What was his early life like? What were some of his earliest inventions? What was his favorite invention?

Africa

- **African Housing**—Construct a series of models to show the various kinds of traditional housing found in different parts of Africa. Identify the geographic region or ethnic group associated with each housing type.

- **Africa Game**—Create a board game using the theme of colonial power in Africa, competition for resources, and African nationalism. The object of the game is control of territory.

- **African Masks**—Use papier-mâché or clay to create a mask in the style of a particular African ethnic group. Explain the significance of the mask and how it would be used in a traditional ceremony.

- **Traditional Clothing**—Tie-dye a piece of fabric and use it to create a simple shirt, skirt, or robe.

Latin America

- **Latin America Maps**—Using acetate sheets or tracing paper, prepare a series of maps showing the geography of Latin America, the climate, and the population density. Use the maps to illustrate an oral report on the relationship between geography, climate, and settlement in Latin America.

- **Historic Cuisine**—Prepare a simple meal using foods grown and used by an ancient Latin American civilization, such as the Inca, Maya, or Aztec.

- **Latin American Travelog**—Present a travelog of a Latin American nation, using slides, pictures cut from magazines, travel brochures, or other materials.

- (Group Project) **Amazon Mural**—Create a mural that portrays animals and plants that would be encountered on a journey along the Amazon River.

- (Group Project) **Carnival Celebration**—Dress in appropriate costumes and present a song-and-dance routine in the style of a Brazilian samba club. Make assorted rhythm instruments, such as drums, tambourines, and maracas, to accompany the singing and dancing.

Asia

- **Japanese Screen**—Paint a design on thin fabric or paper and make a miniature Japanese screen. Demonstrate the technique of Japanese painting you used.

- **Japanese Flower Arranging**—Demonstrate the art of *ikebana,* flower arranging, including an explanation of the symbolism of various flowers you are using.

- (Group Project) **Noh Play**—Present a short play in the Japanese Noh tradition, with appropriate masks for the characters.

- (Group Project) **Shadow Puppets**—Create a set of traditional Chinese shadow puppets and a small shadow theater. Present a shadow play.

Europe

- **Relief Map**—Create a relief map of Europe, showing major mountain ranges, rivers, and other land and water features.

- **Medieval Castle**—Construct a model of a medieval castle, and describe what it would have been like to live in such a dwelling.

- **Language Map**—Draw a map that shows the various language families represented in Europe, as well as individual languages spoken in the various countries.

- **Gargoyle Design**—Create an original design for a gargoyle and discuss the significance of the gargoyle as decoration on Gothic cathedrals in Europe.

- (Group Project) **European Folk Dances**—Select one or more countries, and present a typical traditional folk dance. Use appropriate props or costumes.

- **Soviet Nationality Map**—Prepare a map of the Soviet Union, showing the distribution of major language or nationality groups. Attach an appropriate symbol of each group to the proper map location. Symbols might include miniature costumes, craft items, or housing.

- (Group Project) **Common Market Debate**—Select a country to represent, and organize a debate on the topic of whether or not your country should join, or remain a member of, the European Community (European Common Market).

Industrial Revolution

- **(Group Project) Industrial Revolution Debate**—Organize a debate to discuss the pros and cons of the Industrial Revolution. Team members can be divided into two groups—factory workers and owners, for example, and each team should dress in appropriate costumes for their positions. Use posters, models, and other devices as propaganda tools to support your position.

- **Industrial Revolution Time Line**—Create an illustrated time line, highlighting major events and milestones of the Industrial Revolution.

Project Ideas for Science

Earth Science

- **Niagara Falls Model**—Prepare a model or chart of Niagara Falls, showing how erosion has affected the appearance of the falls over the years.

- **Continental Drift Puzzle**—Make a jigsaw puzzle of the world out of wood or heavy cardboard to illustrate the principles of plate tectonics. Use the puzzle as a visual aid for a presentation on continental drift.

- **Desert Terrarium**—Fill a shallow dish with sand and create a miniature desert environment with cactus plants and miniature animal figures that you have made yourself or purchased.

- **Jungle Terrarium**—Use a large jar, bottle, or glass vase to create a miniature jungle with ferns and other appropriate plants. Also use miniature animal figures that represent jungle wildlife.

- **Ocean Farm**—Build an aquarium "farm" to show how the ocean floor can be used for food production.

- **Instant Fossils**—Press shells, leaves, insects, and other items into plaster of Paris or clay to create a set of instant fossils.

Solar System

- **Sundial Model**—Build a model of a sundial, and tell how it works.

- **Visit to the Sun**—You have just returned from a visit to the sun. Give a firsthand account of your trip, and present a slide show using original drawings, magazine illustrations, or photographs that you have prepared as slides.

- **Stonehenge Model**—Create a model of Stonehenge, and tell how it might have been used as an astronomical calendar.

- (Group Project) **Scientists' Dialogue**—Dramatize an imaginary conversation between Ptolemy and Nicolaus Copernicus, climaxing with Copernicus's rejection of Ptolemy's notion that the earth is the center of the universe.

Animals

- **Animal Believe-It-Or-Not**—Compile a list of interesting or unusual facts about animals. Include drawings or photographs where appropriate. Put your facts together in a notebook, or use them to create a series of posters to decorate your classroom.

- **Endangered Species Map**—Select one or more endangered species, and create a map showing how the animal's native habitat has changed over the years.

- **Animal Time Line**—Create an illustrated time line on the evolution of animal life from earliest times.

- **Protective Coloration**—Make a model of an animal that demonstrates the characteristics of protective coloration. Paint an appropriate background setting in which to display the animal to show the effectiveness of the animal camouflage.

Chemistry

- **Water Molecule Model**—Construct a model of a water molecule, and accompany it with a chart telling the percentage of water present in various things such as the human body, the earth, apples, and rocks.

- **Chemistry Construction Game**—Create a game based on the concept of building molecules from atoms. Players compete to accumulate the parts needed to build atoms of various elements, then join them to form molecules of chemical compounds.

- **Chemistry and Photography**—Present a demonstration or lecture on the role of chemistry in photography. Use your own original photographs or drawings as visual aids.

Plants

- **Leaf Tour**—Conduct a "guided tour" of the outside and inside of a leaf, pointing out the various points of interest along the way. Use slides or a series of posters to illustrate your comments.

- **The Many Faces of Soybeans**—Create a display showing the various items made from soybeans (or corn, or peanuts, or cotton), and use it for a presentation describing the processes used to transform the raw material into the finished products.

- **Mold Farm**—Make a mold "farm" with fields of various kinds of molds grown on assorted food mediums.

Cells

- **Cell Tour**—Create a series of travel posters or slides to illustrate a tour through a typical cell. Include information about the functions of various structures you encounter during your tour.

Human Body

- **Human Body Measurements**—Prepare an illustrated chart that answers such questions as: How many square feet of skin are there in an average adult? How many quarts of blood? How many miles of blood vessels? How big is a red blood cell? How much does an adult brain weigh? How much does a heart weigh? How many feet of intestines does a person have?

- **Germ Travelog**—Portray a germ describing its travels from one place to another and finally into a human body. Illustrate your travelog with slides or pictures cut from magazines.

- **Disease vs. Human Body**—Present a ringside, blow-by-blow radio account of a fight between a disease-causing organism and the human body's defense system.

Universe

- **Biography of a Star**—Present an oral biography of a star, from birth to death, accompanied by a "family album" of illustrations.

- **Miniature Planetarium**—Create a miniature planetarium from an oatmeal box, shoebox, or some other material, showing one or more of the most famous constellations. The viewer should be able to hold the planetarium up to the light, look into one end, and see the constellation, made with pinpricks, at the other end.

Heredity

- **Mendel Mobile**—Create a mobile to illustrate Gregor Mendel's famous experiments on heredity.

Project Ideas for Language Arts

General

- **Almanac History**—Portray Benjamin Franklin as you present an oral report on the history of the almanac. Illustrate your presentation with a drawing of a page from Franklin's own publication, *Poor Richard's Almanac,* or with posters displaying some of his famous sayings that appeared in the almanac.

- **Books Through the Ages**—Depict the history of books by making models of the earliest kinds of books—clay tablets, papyrus scrolls, and hand-sewn books, for example.

- **State Travel Brochure**—Prepare a travel brochure for your state. Include information about geography, climate, places to visit, and special events that tourists might enjoy.

- **Newbery Medal**—Draw or sculpt a model of the Newbery Medal, and present a report about John Newbery and the award named for him. Include a display of several books that have won the Newbery Award.

- **Book Jackets from the 1800's**—Prepare an original design for a book jacket for a famous work of children's literature of the 1800's.

- **English Language Map**—Make a map or series of maps illustrating the development of the English language from various sources (Celts, Germanic and Viking invaders, and Normans).

- **Alphabet History**—Produce a chart tracing the development of the Roman alphabet from Egyptian hieroglyphics and other ancient letter systems.

- **Illuminated Manuscripts**—Prepare a page of text in the style of a medieval illuminated manuscript, using appropriate calligraphy and artwork.

Fairy Tales, Fables, Folklore, and Myths

- **Fairy Tale Characters**—Make a set of stuffed animals or dolls representing characters from a fairy tale by Hans Christian Andersen or the Grimm brothers.

- (Group Project) **Mother Goose Interview**—Present a dramatization of an interview with Mother Goose. Find out about the history of her nursery rhymes, including the origins of some famous nursery rhymes based on real people.

- **Greek Temple**—Construct a miniature temple in honor of the Greek god or goddess of your choice. Decorate the temple with symbols appropriate to the deity.

- (Group Project) **Fable Puppets**—Create a set of puppets based on a selected fable, and present a puppet show dramatizing the fable.

- **Folk Sculptures**—Create a soft sculpture figure to represent a character from American folklore, such as Paul Bunyan or John Henry.

Poetry, Epics, and Ballads

- **Poetry Poster**—Create an illustrated poster of a poem by Robert Louis Stevenson, Emily Dickinson, Robert Frost, or another poet of your choice. Dress in appropriate costume and recite aloud a poem by the poet you have chosen.

- **Ballad Calligraphy**—Prepare a copy of several lines of a ballad or epic in calligraphy, with appropriate colored decorations.

Novels and Short Stories

- (Group Project) **Novel Drama**—Produce and act out a scene from a novel you have read. Include appropriate costumes, scenery, props, and makeup.

- **Dickens Design**—Design a book jacket and type face for a book by Charles Dickens, using a style appropriate to the time of the publication.

- **Poe Presentation**—Design a backdrop to illustrate a story by Edgar Allan Poe, dress as Poe himself might have dressed, and read aloud the story you have chosen.

Drama

- **Drama Masks**—Use papier-mâché or clay to sculpt a pair of classical theatrical masks depicting comedy and tragedy.

- **Elizabethan Theater**—Build a model of an Elizabethan theater, and tell how such theaters differed from modern theaters.

- **Stage Set**—Design a stage set for one particular act or scene of a play by William Shakespeare.

- **Costume Design**—Design and sew a costume for a character in a Shakespeare play.

- **Shakespeare Review**—Portray an Elizabethan critic and present a review of a "new" Shakespeare play you have just seen premiered at the Globe Theatre. Present your review live, or videotape it.

Journalism and Public Opinion

- **Public Service Commercial**—Create a sixty-second radio or TV commercial to promote the idea of using public transportation rather than automobiles for commuting to and from work.

- **Math Ad**—Create and film an advertisement designed to convince students to study math.

- (Group Project) **Class Newspaper**—Prepare one issue of a newspaper about your class. Interview students and teachers for articles, take photos, and draw editorial cartoons. Put the material in newspaper form, and if your school has printing facilities, print the newspaper.

Project Ideas for Math

General

- **Arabic Numerals Map**—Prepare a map showing the origins and spread of Arabic numerals. Use the map as a visual aid for a presentation on the history of Arabic numerals.

- **Climate Averages**—Prepare a chart that shows the high and low temperatures and amount of precipitation in your city or town each day for one month. Calculate the average monthly temperature and precipitation from the figures you have tabulated. Present a report on the climate of your state as a whole, using your city and town figures as part of your information.

- **Scale Models of Trees**—Select at least ten common North American trees, and make paper or cardboard scale models, using the same scale for each tree.

- **Möbius Strip**—Perform a demonstration in which you construct a Möbius strip and show its distinctive features. Tell about August Möbius and his contributions to mathematics.

- **Pi Report**—Tell about the history of pi, including developments by the ancient Egyptians, Chinese, and Greeks, as well as more contemporary mathematicians.

- **Math Time Line**—Create a time line citing major events or milestones in the history of mathematics.

- **Drawing to Scale**—Make a scale drawing of the first floor of your house or apartment.

- **Nutrition Math**—Find out what your recommended daily allowance is for some important food elements, such as protein, carbohydrates, fats, vitamins, and minerals. Keep track of your food intake for a week or more, and use nutrition tables and information on food labels to determine what percentage of your daily requirements you are actually getting in the food you eat.

- **Chinese Puzzle**—Make a Chinese tangram puzzle out of wood or heavy cardboard, and show how all seven pieces can be put together to form a rectangle, a parallelogram, a right triangle, and other shapes.

- **Pyramid Numbers**—Construct a tetrahedron and other three-dimensional models to illustrate the principles of pyramid numbers.

Fractions and Per Cent

- **Equivalent Fractions Mobile**—Create a series of mobiles to illustrate equivalent fractions.

- **Stained Glass Fractions**—Using colored paper, cellophane, or a stained glass kit, create stained glass designs that illustrate various simple fractions.

- **Language Fractions**—Create a chart showing, in both fractions and percentages, the breakdown of language groups throughout the world.

Algebra

- **Algebra Hall of Fame**—Create a set of clay, paper, or cardboard figures to represent persons who made major contributions to the study of algebra over the years.

- **Equation Balance**—Construct a simple balance and a set of "equation blocks" to demonstrate that both sides of an equation must be equivalent.

- **Algebra Origins Map**—Draw a map showing the places where early ideas about algebra were developed. Use it as a visual aid for a presentation about algebra history.

Geometry

- **Color Geometry**—Present a report on the use of geometry in color theory, covering such topics as the color wheel, complementary colors, and triads.

- **Flower Geometry**—Give a demonstration on flower arranging, and point out the geometry involved, both in the shapes of the flowers themselves and in the structure of the overall design. Relevant design elements might include the triangle, symmetry, assymetry, and vertical and horizontal lines.

- **Geometry in Architecture**—Take photographs of buildings that incorporate geometric shapes in an interesting way. Mount your photos on posterboard for a display, or assemble them in a notebook. Present a report on Le Courbusier, I. M. Pei, or some other architect known for using distinctive geometric shapes.

- **Gem Models**—Using colored cellophane or some other appropriate medium, construct models of gemstones cut in various geometric shapes.

- **Crystal Collection**—Collect and display a variety of rocks and minerals to illustrate prisms and various other solid geometric forms.

- **Perspective Design**—Use perspective to design and draw a three-dimensional portrayal of a building with a variety of geometric shapes. Give a demonstration showing the first steps involved in creating the design.

- **Model City**—Using cones, cylinders, cubes, and other solid shapes, create a model of the downtown area of your hometown or an imaginary town.

- **Cubism**—Present a report and demonstration on the painting style of cubism. Show how a cubist painter might transform a traditional still life or landscape into a series of geometric shapes.

- **Pythagoras Teaches Math**—Dress in appropriate costume to portray the ancient Greek mathematician Pythagoras, and teach your class the Pythagorean theorem. Also present a demonstration about figurate numbers and other interesting math ideas developed by the Pythagoreans.

Graphs

- **Budget Pies**—Prepare a personal budget for yourself, showing income from allowance and other earnings, and planned expenditures. Prepare two pie charts, or circle graphs, to show the distribution of your income and expenditures.
- **State Population Graphs**—Prepare a series of graphs about the population of your state. Prepare a line graph showing population growth since the 1800's, a circle graph showing the breakdown of urban/rural population, and a bar graph showing the populations of the five largest cities or towns.

How can you grab and hold onto your audience's attention during your presentation? This section gives several techniques on how to use attention getters.

Where to Use Them	**114**
A Sampler of Attention Getters	**116**

Attention Getters

Would you like to be a straight-A student—
without ever having to study? Would you like
to find out how it can be done?

Well, unfortunately, this book does not have the formula. What those questions were designed to do was to arouse your interest—to serve as an attention getter. Attention getters are devices you can use to arouse and keep your audience's interest during your presentation.

In Section II, you learned that when you give a presentation, you should have two goals in mind: to convey information clearly and to hold the interest of the audience from start to finish. Attention getters are designed to help you reach the second goal. But they also play a role in helping you to reach the first goal—conveying information. How? Simple. If the audience loses interest in your presentation, they may tune out, and the information you are trying to share will never be received. In other words, achieving the first goal may depend on how well you do in achieving the second goal.

Questions such as the ones that opened this section can be effective attention getters. Other devices that you can use include anecdotes, quotations, startling facts and statistics, word pictures, audience participation, and special effects.

Where to Use Them

Attention getters can be used effectively in all parts of your presentation. With careful planning, you can include them in your introduction, in the body of your presentation, and in the conclusion.

In the Introduction

Remember that one of the chief purposes of your introduction is to snare the audience—to make them eager to hear what you plan to say. An attention getter can play a critical role here.

If you succeed in making your audience sit up and look interested, it is not only good for them, it is also good for you. The positive feedback you get from an interested audience will help inspire you to continue your presentation with enthusiasm and confidence. It will help you get over the feelings of nervousness you may have felt before you got up to speak.

In the Body

What good does it do to grab the audience's attention at the start of your presentation if you cannot hold onto it? You don't want to start off with a bang and then leave your audience disappointed with the rest of what you have to say. That is why attention getters also belong in the body of your presentation. They can keep the audience alert and involved during that long period of time between your introduction and your conclusion.

In the Conclusion

When you reach the end of your presentation, you don't just say, "Well, that's all I've got to say," or "That's the end of my presentation." You should briefly summarize the points you made earlier and then leave the audience with something that will make a lasting impression. An attention getter is the device that can help you make that lasting impression.

A Word of Caution

Even though attention getters can have a place in any part of your presentation, don't overdo it. Any device loses its effectiveness if it is used over and over again. Instead, sprinkle attention getters here and there, wherever you think your presentation could use a boost. There are enough different kinds of attention getters that you should be able to pick and choose without overdoing any single variety.

Be sure to work attention getters into your presentation in a smooth, well-planned manner. Don't drop them in abruptly without having them relate in some way to the information you present just before or afterwards.

A Sampler of Attention Getters

Be sure to work attention getters into your presentation in a smooth, well-planned manner.

Because there are so many different kinds of attention getters, you should have no trouble finding at least a few that are appropriate for your particular presentation. The following examples should give you some ideas about how to use attention getters effectively. As you read through them, you may come across some that you can adapt for your own use.

Anecdotes

Anecdotes are brief stories. Most people love to listen to a good story, so if you can present information in an interesting narrative form, your audience is highly likely to pay attention. An anecdote can be a historical account involving a famous person, or it can be something you tell about your own experiences. It can be serious or humorous. Just make sure your anecdote is relevant to your topic.

Here is an example of an anecdote that enhanced a presentation about ancient Inca architecture:

> More than 75 years ago, an American professor named Hiram Bingham was traveling in the Andes Mountains in Peru, in search of Inca ruins. He asked an Indian man that he met if the man knew of any ruins. The Indian said yes, and pointed to the top of a huge mountain. He agreed to lead Bingham to the ruins. They traveled together for two hours in a cold drizzle, struggling through the forest and up a long slope. To climb the steepest parts, they used logs with notches cut into them as ladders. If the men lost their footing, they would have fallen down the mountain into the rushing river below.

Finally, they saw a man and a young boy at work in a field that had been cut into the mountainside. The boy led Bingham to an ancient deserted city between two mountain peaks, about 8,000 feet above sea level. There, Bingham saw the ruins of a temple, a large staircase, an altar to a sun god, and many houses. The young boy had led Bingham to the lost city of Machu Picchu—one of the most spectacular Inca sites ever found.

Here is an example of a personal anecdote a student used in a science presentation about choking and the lifesaving technique called the Heimlich maneuver:

I first learned about the Heimlich maneuver in a frightening way. I was at a restaurant with my family, celebrating my sister's twelfth birthday. We were laughing and enjoying our steak dinners, when all of a sudden my dad sat back and put his hand to his throat. He couldn't breathe or talk, and within a few seconds, he started to turn blue.

My mom jumped up to try to help him but didn't know what to do. We were all in a panic. People at the next table rushed over and started yelling for help. In a few seconds, a waiter ran to our table and grabbed my dad out of my mother's arms. He used the Heimlich maneuver, and in an instant, a piece of steak popped out of my dad's mouth. He was exhausted, but all right. If it hadn't been for that waiter and the Heimlich maneuver, my dad probably would have died within a few minutes.

Both of these anecdotes added an element of drama and true-life adventure to the presentations in which they were used. They conveyed information in a way that kept the audience interested.

Questions

Questions are a way to get the audience involved in your presentation, to get them actively thinking about your topic instead of just passively sitting and listening to you. Questions also can be an effective way to achieve a relaxed, conversational tone in your presentation.

Some questions you ask are rhetorical. That is, you don't actually expect an answer from the audience. For example, in a presentation about pigments in leaves, you might ask, "Have you ever wondered why some leaves turn yellow in autumn, and others turn red or orange?"

You can also ask questions that the audience is actually expected to respond to, with either a show of hands, a "yes" or "no," or some other response. For example, you can ask their opinions on a particular topic:

> How many of you believe that live animals should be used for medical research?

You can take an informal survey:

> How many of you watch television less than one hour a day? One to three hours? More than three hours?

You can ask your audience to guess a statistic:

> How many kinds of insects do you think there are?

When you ask a question, be sure that you are prepared to react to whatever response your audience makes. Also, be sure to keep control over the situation. Don't let audience responses turn into a free-for-all discussion. Resume your presentation immediately after acknowledging the audience's response to your question.

Don't let audience responses turn into a free-for-all discussion.

Startling Facts or Statistics

Most people enjoy hearing bits of believe-it-or-not information. Startling facts or statistics fall into this category. They arouse interest because the audience experiences a sense of surprise or amazement, and they lend a dramatic touch to a presentation.

To be effective, the information should be generally unknown to the audience. For example, it could be argued that the fact that the sun is about 93 million miles away from the earth qualifies as a startling statistic. But if you include that fact in a presentation to your science classmates, all of whom have been studying the solar system, it will make little or no impression.

Here is an example of one way to present a startling fact. It is an introduction for a presentation about a science project that studied the poisons contained in various kinds of flowers:

> Take a look at this bouquet of flowers. They're beautiful, aren't they? They're also deadly. Every one of these flowers contains a poison that can make you seriously ill, or even kill you.

A startling statistic enlivened this student's presentation on caterpillars:

> Few of us think of the caterpillar as a superior being. But there's one category in which the caterpillar comes out far ahead of humans: muscles. We humans have fewer than seven hundred muscles in our bodies. But caterpillars have between two thousand and four thousand.

Both of these examples arouse audience interest because they say something unexpected. If your topic includes startling facts or statistics, work them into the presentation in a way that takes advantage of their dramatic impact.

Word Pictures

A word picture is like a visual aid that members of the audience create in their own minds from the words you speak. This audience involvement is why a word picture works as an attention getter.

Word pictures can be used in a variety of ways. One of the best ways to use them is to establish a mood at the start of a presentation, as in this example from a presentation on the Pilgrims:

> Imagine yourself in a wooden sailing ship, about 90 feet long, with about 130 other people. You've been on this ship for more than 60 days, sailing on the Atlantic Ocean. You've had no chance to bathe, except with sea water, and your clothes are torn and dirty. You've eaten nothing but salted meat or fish, hard biscuits, and dry cheese. At night, you and about 80 fellow passengers sleep on the floor below the main deck, where there's hardly any air or light.

The ship tosses and rolls, and many of the people around you have been seasick or ill with fevers.

Welcome aboard! You're on the *Mayflower,* and you're a Pilgrim bound for the New World.

Word pictures can be especially effective in making incredible statistics more comprehensible. Consider, for example, the following information about the size of the sun compared to other objects in the solar system:

> The sun is the largest object by far in our solar system. The diameter of the sun is about 865,000 miles, and the diameter of the earth at the equator is only about 7,900 miles. The moon is less than a third the size of the earth, with a diameter of about 2,160 miles. The sun is even bigger than Jupiter, the largest planet. Jupiter has a diameter at its equator of about 88,700 miles.

Chances are, even if your audience pays close attention to what you're saying, they won't quite grasp the relationships being presented, and it is unlikely they will remember the specific statistics. Now see how these facts can be presented as a word picture:

> If the sun were the size of a skyscraper, the earth would be the size of a person. The moon would be the size of a cocker spaniel standing next to the person. Jupiter, the largest planet, would be the size of a small building.

With this word picture in mind, members of your audience will have a better understanding of the information presented, and they are more likely to remember it.

Word pictures can be especially effective in making incredible statistics more comprehensible.

Audience Participation

Attention getters such as questions and word pictures involve the audience in a presentation in an indirect way. You can also actively involve members of the audience by using audience participation. This is a technique that professional entertainers sometimes use to increase audience interest and enthusiasm. If you are demonstrating a Greek folk dance, you can invite one or two members of the audience to come up and do it with you, provided it's easy to learn. If you are presenting information about the relationship between exercise and heart rates, you can ask for audience volunteers to come up and have their heart rates measured before and after exercising.

If you are planning on including audience participation as part of your presentation, it might be wise to arrange ahead of time to have at least one or two people who will be willing to participate if no one else volunteers. Otherwise, your presentation could be stopped short for lack of participants.

Special Effects

Certain presentations lend themselves to the use of special effects. Special effects may involve sound, such as playing a tape of tropical bird calls during a travelog describing a trip along the Amazon River; or they may be visual, such as using a strobe light during a dramatization presented in the style of a silent movie.

In some cases, it is a good idea to clear your special effects with your teacher first. One student began her presentation on a murder mystery by Edgar Allan Poe by letting out a blood-curdling scream. Fortunately, she had informed the teacher first and closed all the windows and doors.

Quotations

Quotations lend an air of authority to a presentation. If you use a quotation from a well-known person, it adds strength to the information you have presented, so that the audience is more likely to accept it. Quotations can be especially effective in the conclusion of a presentation, when you want to leave your audience with something to think about. Here is an example of a quotation used at the end of a presentation dealing with air pollution:

Quotations lend an air of authority to a presentation.

> Air pollution is a problem that could threaten the very existence of the earth as we know it. We must find solutions. The astronomer Carl Sagan has put it this way: "Are we

willing to tolerate ignorance and complacency in matters that affect the entire human family? Do we value short-term advantages above the welfare of the earth? Or will we think on longer time scales, with concern for our children and our grandchildren, to understand and protect the complex life-support systems of our planet? The earth is a tiny and fragile world. It needs to be cherished."

Quotations need not be serious and weighty to be effective. Sometimes they simply provide an insightful human interest factor to a presentation. The following introduction to a presentation on the novel *Huckleberry Finn* uses a quote from Mark Twain about the book:

> In a letter to one of his editors, Mark Twain wrote, "I have written 400 pages on it—therefore it is very nearly half done. It is Huckleberry Finn's Autobiography. I like it only tolerably well, as far as I have got, and may possibly pigeonhole it or burn the [manuscript] when it is done."

Quotations can also inject a bit of humor into a presentation, such as this one worked into a presentation about observing comets:

> People who decide to try to observe comets need a good deal of patience. One of the most famous comets, Halley's comet, only appears in the sky once every 75 years or so. People who missed seeing it in 1986 can try again in the year 2061, but science fiction writer Isaac Asimov thinks it will be even better in 2138. According to Asimov, ". . . if we can all hang on for another 150 years we'll see a really good show."

If you use a quotation, take care to tie it neatly into your presentation with relevant introductory remarks.

If you use a quotation, take care to tie it neatly into your presentation with relevant introductory remarks. Also, unless you are certain that the person you are quoting is well known to everyone in your audience, include an identifying phrase before the person's name, such as "the astronomer Carl Sagan" or "the science fiction writer Isaac Asimov."

A Few Final Words

Some attention getters, such as quotations, emerge as a result of your research. But others are simply the result of your own creative thinking. Try to look at the material in your presentation from various angles to see how it can be made most interesting to your audience. Use whatever devices seem appropriate for your purpose, but don't overdo it. If a device seems awkward, or you are uncomfortable with it, don't use it.

Remember that attention getters are devices to help you make the most out of the information you have to share with your audience. They will not save a presentation that is short on information. But they will make a good presentation even better. They will help to keep your audience interested in what you have to say; if you have accomplished that, you can congratulate yourself for having given a successful presentation.

Index

A

Africa (project ideas), 98
Agencies, 30–31
    as source of audio–visual
      aids, 39
Algebra (project ideas), 109
American history (project
    ideas), 95–96
American Indians (project
    ideas), 93–94
Ancient civilization (project
    ideas), 97
Anecdotes, 35, 116–117
Animals (project ideas), 102
Art Index, 25
Asia (project ideas), 99
Associations, 31
    as source for audio–visual
      aids, 39
Attention getters, 35, 112–123
    samples, 116–123
    where to use them,
      114–116
Audiences, 20–21
    age, 20–21
    educational level, 20–21
    familiarity with topic, 21
    participation, 35, 120–121
    question-answer session,
      85–86
    reaction, 84–85
    size, 21
    trouble with, 88
Audio–visual aids, 36–44
    dramatizing a point, 37
    as learning aid, 37
    list of suggestions, 67
    making effective, 38–39
    making your own, 40
    providing examples, 38
    ready made, 39
    rehearsing with, 67–74
    setting a mood, 38
    tips, 67–68
    trouble with, 88

Availability of materials, 19

B

Background information, 21
Background knowledge, 18
Ballads (project ideas), 106
Bar graphs, 44
Body language, 60–66
Business associations, 31; *See
    also* Associations

C

Call numbers, 24
Card catalog, 23–24
Cells (project ideas), 103
Charts, 40–42
Chemistry (project ideas), 103
Circle graphs, 44
Clarity of pronunciation, 59–60
Classification chart, 40–41
Communication skills, 12, 13
Computer-assisted research, 27
Computerized catalog, 23
Creativity, 11–12, 123

D

Delivery formats, 51–57
    memorizing presentation,
      53–55
    reading from manuscript,
      51–53
    speaking
      extemporaneously,
      55–57
Developing projects, 16–47;
    See also Projects
    choosing topic, 17–20
    determining purpose,
      21–22
    planning, 16–17
Dewey Decimal Classification
    System, 24

Drama (project ideas), 107
Drawing, 28

E

Earth science (project ideas),
  101
Encyclopedia of Associations,
  31
Energy level, 60
Entertaining projects, 22
Epics (project ideas), 106
Equipment; *See also* Audio–
  visual aids
      trouble with, 88
Eskimos (project ideas), 94
Europe (project ideas), 99–100
Eye contact, 64; *picture,* 65

F

Fables (project ideas), 106
Facial expressions, 63
Fairy tales (project ideas), 106
Feedback, 84–85
Filmstrip projector, 71
Flip charts, 42
Flow charts, 42; *picture,* 43
Folklore (project ideas), 106
Fractions (project ideas), 109

G

Geometry (project ideas),
  110–111
Gestures, 66; *picture,* 66
Goals, 32
Government agencies, 30–31;
  See also Agencies
Graphs, 42, 44
Graphs (project ideas), 111
Group projects, 45–47
      keeping on track, 46
      rehearsing, 46
      responsibility, 46

H

Heredity (project ideas), 104

Human body (project ideas),
  104

I

Ideas for projects, 90–111; *See
  also specific subjects*
      language arts, 105–108
      math, 108–111
      science, 101–104
      social studies, 93–100
Industrial Revolution (project
  ideas), 100
Information services, 27
      writing for information,
      30–31
Informative projects, 21
Interests, 11–12, 18
Interviews, 28; *picture,* 29
Inventions (project ideas),
  97–98

J, K

Journalism (project ideas),
  107–108

L

Language arts (project ideas),
  105–108
Latin America (project ideas),
  98–99
Learning aids, 37
Library, 22–27
      services, 27
      as source of audio–visual
      aids, 39
Library catalogs, 23–24
Line graphs, 42
Local agencies, 31
Long-term benefits (of
  projects), 13

M

Map and globe skills (project
  ideas), 97
Math (project ideas), 108–111

Memorizing presentation,
    53–55
Memory tips, 54–55
Microfilm, 23
Mishaps, 87
*Monthly Catalog of United
    States Government
    Publications,* 31
Mood, 38
Myths (project ideas), 106

N

Nervousness, 81–84
Newspaper indexes, 25–26
New York Times, 26
New York Times Index, 25
Nonfiction books, 22–23, 24
Novels (project ideas),
    106–107

O

Observation, 27–28
Online database systems, 27
Opaque projector, 69
Oral report, 32
Organization (of presentation),
    31–37
Organization chart, 40
Organizing skills, 12
Outlines, 35–36
    for delivery, 56–57
Overhead projector, 70

P

Pamphlets, 28
Per cent (project ideas), 109
Periodical indexes, 25–26
Personal appearance, 80–81
Persuasive projects, 22
Picture graphs, 44
Pitch, 59
Plants (project ideas), 103
Poetry (project ideas), 106
Posture, 62
Presentation, 10–13, 31–47
    check list, 47

final review, 76–77
four rules, 89
goals, 32
judging content, 58
kinds of, 32
making, 78–89
organizing, 31–36
pinpointing purpose, 33
presentation site, 75–76
Professional associations, 31;
    See also Associations
Projects; *See also* Developing
    projects
    check list, 47
    and developing skills,
        12–13
    development of, 16–47
    group, 45–47
    ideas, 90–111
    as learning tools, 11
    long-term benefits, 13
    presentation, 10–13
    purpose of, 10–12
    tapping interest and
        creativity, 11–12
Pronunciation, 59–60
Props, 36–44, 67–74
    dramatizing a point, 37
    as learning aid, 37
    list of suggestions, 67
    making effective, 38–39
    making your own, 40
    providing examples, 38
    ready made, 39
    rehearsing with, 67–74
    setting a mood, 38
    tips, 67–68
    trouble with, 88
Public opinion (project ideas),
    107–108
Purpose, 10–12, 21–22
    pinpointing, 33

Q

Question-answer sessions,
    85–86

Questions (as attention getters), 114, 117–118
Quotations, 35, 121–122

R

Readers' Guide to Periodical Literature, 25; *picture,* 25
Reading from manuscript, 51–53
Readings
    preparing manuscript, 52–53
Reading techniques, 52
Record player, 74
Reference books, 24
Reference service, 27
Reference works, 23
Rehearsing, 48–77
    delivery format, 51–57
    step-by-step approach, 57–66
Research, 22–31
    library, 22–27
    skills, 12
Reserving books, 23

S

Schedules, 17
Setting up, 80
Short stories (project ideas), 106–107
Site of presentation, 75–76
Skills, 12–13
Slide projector, 68
Sloppy speech habits, 60
Socialization skills, 13
Social studies ideas, 93–100
Solar system (project ideas), 102
Speaking extemporaneously, 55–57
Speaking skills, 12–13
Special effects, 121
Speed, 59
Stage fright, 81–84
    strategies, 82–84
    symptoms, 81–82

Startling facts or statistics, 118–119
State agencies, 31; *See also* Agencies
State history, geography, and economics (project ideas), 93
Statistics, 35, 118–119
Structure, 34–35
Subject index, 24

T

Tables, 40
Talents, 18–19
Tape recorder, 73
Technical language, 20
Technology (project ideas), 97–98
Telephone information service, 27
Three-part structure, 34–35
Time allotments, 19–20
    for presentation, 20
    for project, 19–20
Time lines, 40
Tours, 27–28
Trial run, 75

U

Universe (project ideas), 104
U.S. government agencies, 30–31; *See also* Agencies

V

Vertical file, 25
Videotape player, 72
Vocabulary, 20
Voice, 58–60
Volume, 58–59

W, X, Y, Z

Word pictures, 119–120